FASHION
ファッション＆カラー
total fashion color coordinate
& COLOR

FASHION & COLOR
by Kojiro Kumagai
Copyright © 1985 by Graphic-sha Publishing Co., Ltd.
1-9-12 Kudan-Kita, Chiyoda-ku, Tokyo, Japan
ISBN4-7661-0351-3

はじめに

ライフスタイルも、多情報化、コンピュータ時代になり、あらゆる
自分の知りたい事、欲しい物が、ボタン一つで動かずに手にはいっ
たり、知る事が出来る様になり、衣・食・住すべてのライフスタイ
ルもファッション化して来ました。

色の流行と言えば、ファッションの世界だけと思われていましたが、
今では、自動車、電気製品、インテリアとあらゆるすべてのものに
色という流行が、ターゲットのポイントになって来ました。又それ
と共に、色の組み合わせの感覚が重要視されてきたことも確かです。

今までにない色彩感覚の勉強になるようにこの本は、誰にでも一目
で理解できるように、ファッションイラストによって図解し、色の
コーディネーションを基本的な組み合わせから個性的な組み合わせ
まで、同じ色で、セクシー モダン、フェミニン、カジュアル、ス
ポーティとコスチュームに分け、洋服の色から、メイク、アクセサ

リーまでトータル的に色の組み合わせをしております。

洋服だけに限らず、色を選ぶ時、自分の好みの色を選んでしまいま
す。この選び方が、いちばん無難で抵抗なく受け入れられるからで
しょう。しかし、時には、冒険をし、今まで使った事のない色で組
み合わせて見れば、また新しい発見ができ、おもわぬ感動にぶつか
るものです。そのような感動をこの本で、あなたなりに見つけてみ
て下さい。

昔は色の組み合わせにおいて、タブーとされた色などがありました
が、最近では、どのような色でも分量によって上手に組み合わせて
使いこなしています。
色のコーディネーションのテキストとしてこの本は、参考になるも
のと確信しております。この本を手にして、自分の感覚を磨いて下
さい。

PROLOGUE

The computer has brought with it the information age. Almost whatever information we want can be had at the touch of a button. With this have come many changes and choices, bringing fashion into nearly every aspect of our food, our clothing, and our homes.

The subject of color was once thought of as limited to the world of fashion. But now it has become an important selling point for our cars, electrical appliances, and interiors; touching nearly every aspect of our lives. At the same time, a lot more importance is being given to color combinations.

It is clear that a whole new color sense has emerged, and this book is designed to help anyone understand these new color schemes at a glance. The fashion illustrations included in this book help clarify everything from basic color coordination, to combinations which express your individual taste. The color combinations in clothing, make-up, and accessories are covered in a total approach to color fashion. Using the one color,

you can create the four styles such as sexy & modern, feminine, casual, sporty from this book.

Frequently not only in clothing, but in other areas of your lifestyle, you choose colors according to your own taste. This method of choosing is the easiest to accept, and the least likely to cause problems. However, sometimes you want to experiment, and try something a little daring. Out of a sense of adventure, you may want to try a new color that you've never tried before. Sometimes a new discovery can be surprisingly right. And this book can help you make these discoveries.

Some color combinations were taboo in the past. But by skillfully mixing colors in the right amounts, almost any color can be used to produce a pleasing effect.

This is a basic reference for color coordination. With this book at hand, you will have a confidence in your choices. And as you use it, you will find that it sharpens your own sense for color coordination.

目　次
Contents

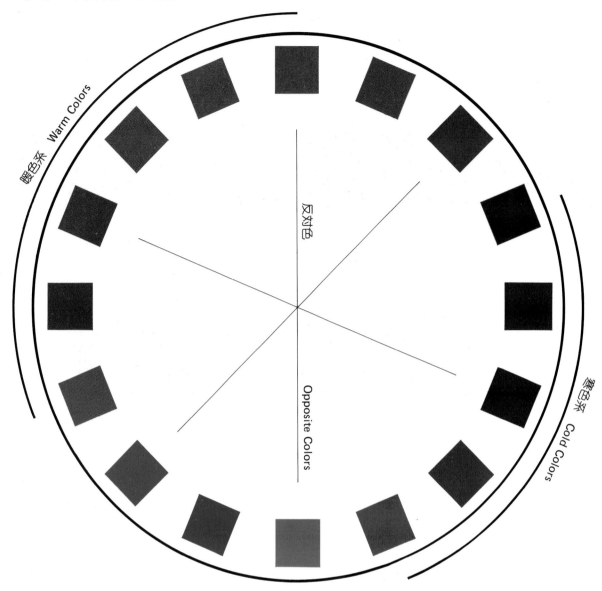

暖色系 Warm Colors

寒色系 Cold Colors

反対色 Opposite Colors

有彩色（色相環）

有彩色は基本的に、赤、橙、黄、黄緑、緑、青緑、青、青紫、紫、赤紫の10色相に分けられ、それを順に環にしたものを色相環といい、暖色系、寒色系、反対色と色わけすることもできます。その色の組み合わせによって、色のイメージを言葉にすることができます。このような図を利用すれば、カラーコーディネイトする場合に役立ちます。

Colors (Color Hue)

Colors are basically divided into 10 hues – red, orange, yellow, yellow-green, green, blue-green, blue, violet, purple, and magenta.   Arranged in this order on a wheel forming what is called a color wheel, they can be broadly categorized into warm, cold, and opposite colors. By combining the colors it is possible to express the image of the color. Such color charts are especially helpful in color co-ordination.

無彩色

有彩色にない、白、グレー、黒などを言います。この色は有彩色のどんな色ともうまく組み合わせることができます。

Monotones

White, gray, and black which have no coloring are called Noncolors. With these noncolors it is possible to combine them with any color.

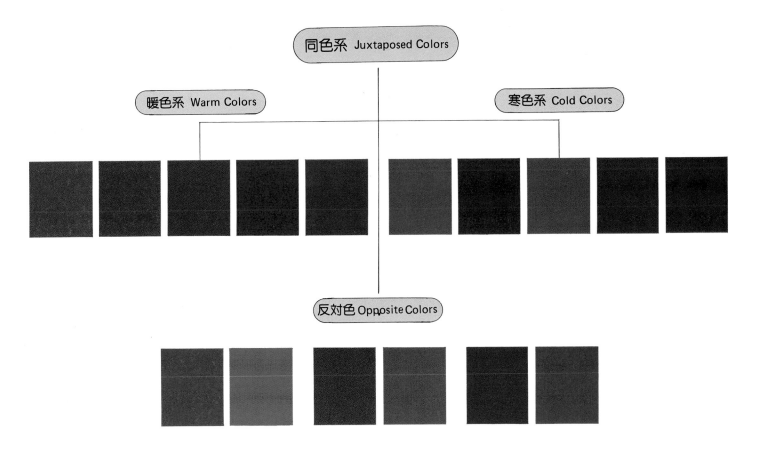

同色系 Juxtaposed Colors

暖色系 Warm Colors

寒色系 Cold Colors

反対色 Opposite Colors

左ページの色相環を同系色、反対色、暖色系、寒色系にわかりやすくしたものです。
It is easy to categorize the color wheel on the left page into juxtaposed, opposite, warm, and cold colors.

反対色──

色相環で相対する色を反対色と言います。
反対色は、バランスがとりやすく組み合わせには問題はありませんが、イメージとしては強く（派手）見える配色になります。

Opposite Colors ─

Colors that are symmetrically opposite each other on the color wheel are called Opposite Colors. As Opposite Colors are easy to balance, there are no problems involved when combining them, however, imagewise the color schemes appear strong (flashy).

行動的
Vibrant

粋な
Elegant

シャープ
Sharp

同系色の組み合わせ

暖色系──

色相で、赤、橙、黄の系統を暖色と言います。

暖色系は、生き生きとして暖かい感じを人に与え、興奮感をもっています。また豪華さがあり、華やかな雰囲気があります。

Juxtaposed Colors Combinations

Warm Colors —

Hues consisting of reds, oranges, and yellows are called Warm Colors. Radiating a vibrant warmth, Warm Colors act as stimulators. Luxurious, as well, they have a rich, gorgeous atmosphere surrounding them.

晴れやか
Cheerful

可愛さ
Pretty

女性的
Feminine

寒色系──

色相で、青緑、青、青紫の系統を寒色と言います。

寒色系は、涼しい、寒いといった感じを与え沈静感をもっています。組み合わせには、冷たくシンプルな感じになりやすく、シャープで知的なイメージには効果的です。

Cold Colors —

Hues consisting of blue-greens, blues, and violets are called Cold Colors. Possessing a cool/cold feeling they have a tranquilizing effect. When combined together, they are apt to project a simple, cold sensation. Sharp, they are effective in giving off an intellectual image.

新鮮
Fresh

清楚
Neat

さわやか
Clean

FASHION & COLOR

sexy modern セクシーモダン

網点パーセント表示は、C（シアン）、M（マゼンタ）、Y（イエロー）、BL（ブラック）の順です。

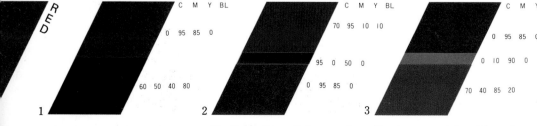

	C	M	Y	BL
1	0	95	85	0
	60	50	40	80

	C	M	Y	BL
2	70	95	10	10
	95	0	50	0
	0	95	85	0

	C	M	Y	BL
3	0	95	85	0
	0	10	90	0
	70	40	85	20

RED

1. 情熱のあふれた力強い組み合わせ。
2. 古式ゆかしい中に、気高い僧侶を思わせる。
3. 情熱の中に秘められたシックさが大人っぽい。

A strong, passionate combination.

Traditional, reminiscent of a noble priest.

Passionate, with a hint of chicness and sophistication.

1. やさしい気持ちの中に、強い自分をもって
   いるような雰囲気の色あい。
2. 自信があったら、使ってみたい色。

	C	M	Y	BL
	0	25	20	0
	95	70	0	0
	0	95	85	0

	C	M	Y	BL
	0	95	85	0
	95	10	0	0

1

Carefree and feminine but with a strong sense of individuality.

2

Try this if you have a confidence.

13

	C	M	Y	BL
	0	95	85	0
	90	5	30	0
1	100	50	0	0

	C	M	Y	BL
	55	30	55	15
	0	0	65	0
	40	45	90	15
2	0	95	85	0

	C	M	Y	BL
	20	35	25	0
	0	20	90	0
3	0	95	85	0

1.アメリカ大陸の思い出が、ふとよぎる。

2.難しい仕事をしながらも、楽しい事が待っている。キャリアウーマン向き。

3.あたたかい心でみなに接したい。誰にでも似合わせるのには、難しい。

1 A subtle sense of the American Continent.

2 A sense of enjoyment, even on the job. This is for the career woman.

3 While it conveys a friendly feeling toward everyone you meet. This combination is not for everyone.

1. あたたかい所で、冷たいものを飲んでいる
   みたい。
2. 子供の頃の運動会が思い出される。
3. 外国の国旗にあったよう。分量によって少
   し難しいけれど、大人ぽさがある。

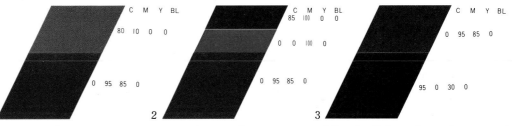

	C	M	Y	BL
	80	10	0	0
	0	95	85	0

1 *Like a cool drink on a warm day.*

	C	M	Y	BL
	85	100	0	0
	0	0	100	0
	0	95	85	0

2 *Reminiscent of a sports day during your childhood.*

	C	M	Y	BL
	0	95	85	0
	95	0	30	0

3 *Like the flying colors of a national flag, this combination is a bit difficult to do well. But in the right amounts, it has a great deal of sophistication.*

	C	M	Y	BL		C	M	Y	BL
	0	90	85	0		85	20	35	20
	80	50	0	0		20	5	0	0
	85	50	20	10		0	90	85	0

L I G H T
R E D

1

Both smart and practical; a nice balance of the dark violet shades of autumn.

2

With a sense of calm refinement, this is a sophisticated color arrangement, with a touch of exotic green.

1. 上・下それぞれ、やさしく甘いカラーどうし。ベルトの紺が全体を引き締めている。
2. モダンな色の組み合わせ。いかにも春らしい、大胆に使ってヤング向き。
3. やわらかく、あたたかい色どうしの組み合わせ。ロマンチックで華やかな感じ。

	C	M	Y	BL
	60	10	30	0
1	0	90	85	0

	C	M	Y	BL
	25	10	60	0
	85	20	40	20
2	0	90	85	0

	C	M	Y	BL
	0	90	85	0
3	0	40	35	0

Both upper and lower, the colors are sweet and easy. The purple belt brings the whole combination together.

A bold combination of modern colors, with a sense of springtime. This match is well suited to the young at heart.

This is a casual and warm color combination, with a bright romantic feeling.

	C	M	Y	BL
	0	90	85	0
	35	85	75	20
	25	50	80	0

1

	C	M	Y	BL
	20	35	25	0
	40	45	50	50
	0	90	85	0

2

1. ドライどうしで大陸的。土の臭いもするが、ココアブラウンでなかなかのおしゃれ。

2. 古典的な甘さが漂うメルヘンチックな色あい。使いやすくおしゃれ。

Both colors are continental and businesslike, but the cocoa brown makes the earth color rather fashionable.

A classical scheme with sweet pastel hues. This combination is both fashionable and easy to use.

太陽がいっぱいといった配色。どちらが主役になっても個性的。スポーティからカジュアルまで、幅広く使える。

A color scheme imbued with the hues of the sun. Whichever one is chosen as the principle color, this combination maintains its character. It can be used in a wide range of situations, from sporty to casual.

	C	M	Y	BL
	0	90	85	0
	35	30	25	10
	0	15	100	0

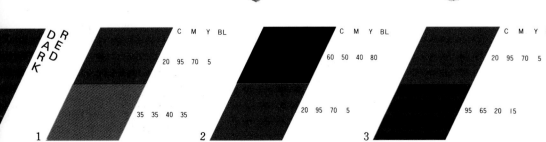

	C	M	Y	BL
1	20	95	70	5
	35	35	40	35

	C	M	Y	BL
2	60	50	40	80
	20	95	70	5

	C	M	Y	BL
3	20	95	70	5
	95	65	20	15

DARK RED

A chic and refined image, suitable for adults.

The yellow and pale brown are brought together in an soft combination.

This is an orthodox color scheme, suited to a young classic look.

1.シックで落ち着いた大人のイメージ。

2.黄色とうす茶が、全体をやさしく引き締めている。

3.オーソドックスなカラーの配色。ヤングクラシック。

1. 類似配色で、落ち着きと優雅な雰囲気を出
   している。オレンジがアクセント。
2. 甘い色の組み合わせ。ヤングアダルト感覚。

	C	M	Y	BL
	20	95	70	5
	60	70	15	10
1	30	30	20	10

	C	M	Y	BL
	0	75	35	0
	35	80	40	20
2	20	95	70	5

Using closely related colors, this color scheme produces a graceful and refined effect, with orange accents.

This color scheme uses sweet hues, suited to a young adult look.

	C	M	Y	BL
	20	95	70	5
	0	35	70	0
	80	25	80	0

1

A warm color arrangement which makes you remind of autumn.

	C	M	Y	BL
	20	95	70	5
	85	0	20	0
	35	35	30	35

2

A classic European harmony.

	C	M	Y	BL
	50	35	90	10
	0	55	95	0
	20	95	70	5

3

A blend of many colors, which combine to create an adult image.

1.秋を思わせるノーブルで温かい配色。
2.クラシックでヨーロッパ調。
3.多色使いだがマッチして、アダルトなイメージをかもし出している。

1.からし色にブルーがマッチして大人ぽい。
2.女性ぽくてグレーが落ち着きをみせている。
3.オレンジ色と草色が赤を引き立てている、
　スポーツ感覚。

C	M	Y	BL
0	40	95	0
95	50	0	0
20	95	70	5

1

A sophisticated combination of blue and mustard color.

C	M	Y	BL
20	95	70	5
40	35	50	40

2

A feminine gray in low tones.

C	M	Y	BL
20	95	70	5
0	60	90	0
50	0	75	0

3

This sporty look springs from an orange and grass-colored scheme, with red highlights.

1.ピンクに対して落ち着きと甘くやさしい配
　色がマッチし、アダルト感覚。
2.個性のある組み合わせ。オリエンタル調。

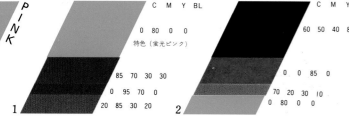

	C	M	Y	BL		C	M	Y	BL
	0	80	0	0		60	50	40	80
特色（蛍光ピンク）									
	85	70	30	30		0	0	85	0
	0	95	70	0		70	20	30	10
1	20	85	30	20	**2**	0	80	0	0

A quiet color scheme for pink. This sweet and tender match is suitable for adults.

This color scheme is vivid and characteristic, in an oriental mood.

1.高価な天然鉱物を思わせる色あい。
2.貴族的な色の組み合わせ。高級感覚。

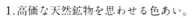
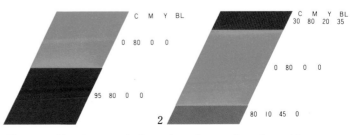

This combination remind us of high-qualified jewelry.

An aristocratic color with a touch of class.

	C	M	Y	BL
	0	80	0	0
1	40	90	20	40

	C	M	Y	BL
	0	80	0	0
	30	0	70	0
2	0	0	40	0

	C	M	Y	BL
	0	80	0	0
3	45	45	80	30

1.あでやかで、エレガント。
2.ナチュラルでやさしい感じ。ちょっと洋風でモダン。
3.カーキ系とはよく合う。ヨーロッパ感覚。

1 *Bright, charming and elegant.*

2 *A natural and soft feeling, in a slightly Western mood.*

3 *This European look goes well with Khaki colors.*

1. 爽やかな季節感。明るくジャンピングカラー。
2. 軽やかな配色で、大人のムード。

	C	M	Y	BL
	0	5	75	0
	40	75	60	55
	0	80	0	0

	C	M	Y	BL
	0	80	0	0
	95	10	0	0
	100	0	70	0

1 *A bright, joyful color, with a refreshing seasonal flavor.*

2 *A light color scheme in an adult mood.*

		C M Y BL			C M Y BL
		0 60 35 0			
					0 60 35 0
		50 0 10 0			
		35 30 20 10			70 90 0 0
					70 25 0 0

SPINK
SALMON

1
A well blended match of dark tones.

2
A scheme of opposing colors, bold but well matched in their own way.

1.ダークトーンの配色をうまく扱っている。
2.反対色の組み合わせ。大胆だがそれなりにマッチする。

1. フルーツカラーがロマンチック。ちょっぴりおきゃんなお嬢さんタイプ。
2. 中間色どうしの組み合わせが、大人ぽい。

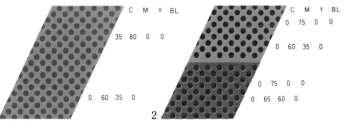

The colors of natural fruit. For young girls with a bit of the tomboy in them.

A neutral color scheme, for an adult look.

		C	M	Y	BL
		0	60	35	0
1		10	100	40	15

		C	M	Y	BL
		0	0	85	0
		95	65	25	15
		15	90	65	0
2		0	60	35	0

		C	M	Y	BL
		0	60	35	0
		55	35	90	5
3		100	0	60	0

1. 甘い色の組み合わせ。ちょっぴり、リッチな色が入って落ち着く。

2. リッチな色との組み合わせに、赤のアクセントで粋なムード。

3. ソフトなグリーンを配して、ハイミセスのイメージ。

A combination of sweet colors, rich and refined.

A stylish mood, created by red accents in a rich color scheme.

This soft green produces a mature, matronly look.

1.甘い色にマッチした個性派の組み合わせ。
2.リッチな感覚の持ち主に最適。

C	M	Y	BL
0	60	35	0
95	90	0	0

1

C	M	Y	BL
0	60	35	0
35	45	95	0

2

A color match in sweet tones, for people with personality.

Perfect for the person with a rich sense of taste.

31

	C	M	Y	BL
	60	50	40	80
	0	90	5	0
1	35	30	20	10

	C	M	Y	BL
	0	90	5	0
	95	90	0	0
2	95	0	65	0

A vivid scheme without color change, creating a stylish mood.

A bright match in three colors. For adults with a sense of independent.

1.無彩色にビビッドな配色で、粋なムード。
2.鮮やかな3色配色。大人のリズムを感じる
　個性派。

1. 鮮やかな色あい。グレーの水玉が抑えになっている大人のムード。
2. ピンクを品よく活かして甘い配色。ヤングアダルト向き。

	C	M	Y	BL
	75	70	65	0
	0	90	5	0

1

	C	M	Y	BL
	0	55	5	0
	35	70	0	0
	0	90	5	0

2

An adult mood created by soft gray dots on a bright background.

A sweet color scheme in pink, with a touch of class. For young adults.

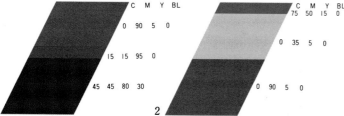

	C M Y BL
	0 90 5 0
	15 15 95 0
	45 45 80 30

1

An olive base, well match-ed with pink and Khaki color.

	C M Y BL
	75 50 15 0
	0 35 5 0
	0 90 5 0

2

This blue color scheme is cute, but not for kids.

1.オリーブ色を主に、ピンクとカーキ色がマッチして。

2.可愛らしさの中に、紺色が大人ぽさを感じさせる。

1.エキゾチックでセクシャルな配色。
2.補色以上に目立つ配色。夏などにぜひ楽し
んで使いたい。

	C	M	Y	BL
1	0	90	50	0
	85	0	85	0

	C	M	Y	BL
2	0	0	90	0
	0	90	50	0

Exotic and sexy.

More than a complimentary color arrangement, these colors will make people stand up and take notice. Just the thing to enjoy summer in.

sexy modern セクシーモダン

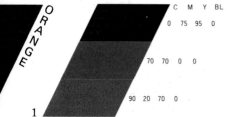

	C	M	Y	BL
	0	75	95	0
	70	70	0	0
	90	20	70	0

	C	M	Y	BL
	0	75	95	0
	85	70	30	25
	20	100	65	5
	40	60	85	0

ORANGE

1.力強く目立つ色あい。3原色に似た効果が
ある。安っぽくならないように効果的に演
出したい。スポーツウエアーにも。

2.暖かみのある類似色でまとめやすいが、全
体では派手。夏のリゾートにも。

1

A striking color match, as effective as three primary colors. Effective enough *to perform in, without looking cheap. Great for sportswear.*

2

A warm scheme in similar colors, with a slightly flashy appearance. Perfect for summer resorts.

36

明るさの中に情熱をおぼえ、暖かさを感じ
ながら大人の女をみる。グリーンがほどよ
く落ち着きをみせて。

C	M	Y	BL
90	0	75	0
0	75	95	0

A bright mood tinged with passion. This color scheme conveys the warmth of a grown woman, yet the touch of green lends a mood of serenity.

		C	M	Y	BL
		0	75	95	0
		0	0	60	0
		25	50	75	0
1		35	70	85	15

		C	M	Y	BL
		85	20	45	5
		55	10	55	0
2		0	75	95	0

1.思いきり気取って大胆に使ってみたい。カ
　ジュアルウエアーからスポーツウエアーに。
2.上下の色あいがぴったりと、かなり目立つ。
　ひすいのような高級感。

*This is a daring match
you'd like to display with
pride, whether in a casual
or sporty situation.*

*A striking match from top
to bottom.   Reminiscent
of expensive jade.*

1. 落ち着いた秋の日、ベージュが加わって大人ぽい色あい。
2. かげがなくドライで色全体が安定。西部の誇りさえも感じる。
3. 太陽がいっぱいといった配色。健康的で、スポーティなイメージカラー。

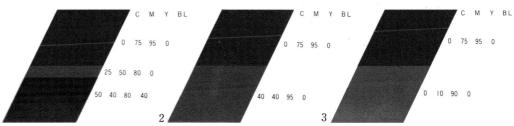

	C	M	Y	BL
	0	75	95	0
	25	50	80	0
1	50	40	80	40

	C	M	Y	BL
	0	75	95	0
2	40	40	95	0

	C	M	Y	BL
	0	75	95	0
3	0	10	90	0

A quiet autumn day, set in adult beige tones.

A dry and stable combination. This color scheme makes you feel a sense of the Western pride.

A color scheme washed in sunshine, with a healthy and sporty image.

sexy modern セクシーモダン

		C M Y BL
		0 45 90 0
		35 70 85 15

1

You can feel comfortable with this combination. Change your mood with this burgundy color scheme.

		C M Y BL
		0 45 90 0
		95 65 20 15

2

A match of opposite colors, good for uniforms.

		C M Y BL
		90 20 70 0
		50 40 35 60
		0 45 90 0

3

A fashionable color blend, with a sense of freshness.

1. 安心して使える組み合わせ。えんじの配色で気分転換。
2. 反対色がマッチして、ユニフォーム効果。
3. ファッショナブルな組み合わせ。鮮度がよい。

1.明度対比がバランスよく、優しさと甘さと
　が若さを出している。

2.コントラストがよく、落ち着いたムード。
　静寂、大きさを感じさせる。

		C	M	Y	BL
		0	45	90	0
		0	65	35	0

1

		C	M	Y	BL
		30	0	45	0
		25	85	35	20
		0	45	90	0

2

A balanced contrast of color value. Sweet, soft, and youthful.

A gentle mood with a nice contrast. Expansive and serene.

41

	C	M	Y	BL
	0	45	90	0
	45	40	70	40
	35	45	95	0

1

	C	M	Y	BL
	0	45	90	0
	10	40	70	0
	25	65	70	0
	70	40	85	20

2

1. 濃淡の組み合わせ。ベルトの色が品のよい
   調和をとる。
2. 暖かく健康的。えんじが引き締め役。スポー
   ティなイメージ。

A scheme of pale and opaque tones. The color of the belt brings about a refined sense of harmony.

A warm sense of vitality, drawn together by the burgundy color. A sporty image.

1. スポーツ感覚。健康的ではつらつと動的。
2. さわやかな色どうしの組み合わせ。
3. 健康的な明るさの中に、大人の落ち着きを。

	C	M	Y	BL
	0	45	90	0
	90	0	80	0
	0	95	70	0

1

A sense of vitality for sportswomen. Vivid and animated.

	C	M	Y	BL
	20	0	50	0
	90	15	75	0
	0	100	75	0
	0	45	90	0

2

A combination of fresh colors.

	C	M	Y	BL
	0	45	90	0
	0	80	90	0
	50	40	90	30

3

Bright and full of vitality, but with a mature look.

sexy modern セクシーモダン

	C	M	Y	BL
	90	75	25	20
	20	90	90	0

1

	C	M	Y	BL
	20	90	90	0
	70	100	5	0

2

	C	M	Y	BL
	90	30	75	0
	60	50	40	80
	20	90	90	0

3

1. 紺のベルトがきいて個性的。
2. 強い色どうしの配色の中に個性がある。
3. 個性の強い色の組み合わせ。黒がドラマチック。

1 A dark blue belt, accented with individuality.

2 A strong sense of individuality, springing from a strong color arrangement.

3 An arrangement of strong individual colors. The black produces a surprising and dramatic effect.

1. 並木道も新芽の息づかいが感じられる。春やわらかく甘味のある色の組み合わせ。
2. 知性のあるバランスのとれた色あい。気品のあるアダルトなイメージ。
3. 抱擁力のあるふくよかな色あい。同系色の組み合わせが上品さをかもしだしている。

	C	M	Y	BL
1	20	0	65	0
	25	50	75	0
	20	90	90	0

	C	M	Y	BL
2	20	90	90	0
	80	50	0	0

	C	M	Y	BL
3	0	40	55	0
	80	60	0	50
	20	90	90	0

Like a stroll down a tree-lined street in the springtime. A soft and sweet color scheme.

Colors matched with an intelligent sense of balance. A refined and mature image.

A generous and full color match. The arrangement of juxtaposed colors creates a sense of refinement.

	C	M	Y	BL
	0	35	65	0
	45	40	70	40
	20	90	90	0

1

	C	M	Y	BL
	20	90	90	0
	0	30	100	0
	95	15	25	20

2

Quiet colors with a sense of warmth. Effectively accented with olive green, for an adult sense of taste.

The opposing colors convey a sense of strength. The added yellow makes it suitable for adults.

1.落ち着きのある色あいで暖かさがあり、オリーブグリーンがきいてアダルト感覚。
2.反対色にみえて力強さを感じさせる。黄色が加わってアダルト向き。

1.スポーツからカジュアルウェアーまで巾広く使える色あい。
2.健康的でスポーティなイメージカラー。

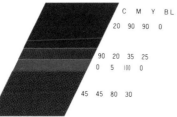

	C	M	Y	BL
	20	90	90	0
	90	20	35	25
	0	5	100	0
	45	45	80	30

From sporty to casual, you can use this color combination almost anywhere.

	C	M	Y	BL
	30	0	75	0
	90	25	30	40
	20	90	90	0

These colors make for a sporty, healthy look.

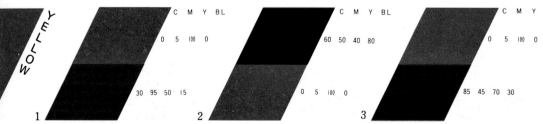

1. イエローのもつ若々しさに深みのあるレッドを加えて、アダルト感覚に。
2. ブラックとイエローの個性的な組み合わせを、グリーンが一層ひきたて上品に。
3. 明度・彩度差が適当で、アダルトなイメージ。深みのある赤が入ることで一層近代感覚に。

	C	M	Y	BL
1	0	5	100	0
	30	95	50	15

	C	M	Y	BL
2	60	50	40	80
	0	5	100	0

	C	M	Y	BL
3	0	5	100	0
	85	45	70	30

1. *A youthful yellow accented by dark red, for an adult mood.*

2. *A combination of black and yellow with a great deal of character. The green gives it an even stronger sense of refinement.*

3. *This is an adult image, with appropriate contrasts of value and hue. And the dark red gives it a still more modern flavor.*

1. イエローに対し反対色の紫を加え、優雅さ
をかもしだしている。
2. 大地のような暖かさ、優しさを感じる色あい。

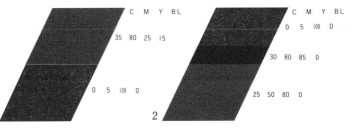

	C	M	Y	BL
	35	80	25	15
	0	5	100	0

	C	M	Y	BL
	0	5	100	0
	30	80	85	0
	25	50	80	0

1 *Yellow against purple creates a feeling of grace.*

2 *The warmth of the earth. This color scheme gives you a relaxed, easy look.*

	C	M	Y	BL
	0	5	100	0
	30	5	70	0
	0	80	50	0

1

A combination of warm colors. Soft and cute, this is a young girl's image.

	C	M	Y	BL
	0	5	100	0
	0	85	10	0
	90	5	10	0

2

This cool and youthful look is for the casual and sporty, with fashionable pink.

	C	M	Y	BL
	60	0	60	0
	0	5	100	0

3

Like a meadow in the springtime, this has a fresh and balmy relaxed feeling to it.

1. ウォームカラーの組み合わせが、ソフトで可愛らしい少女のイメージ。
2. 涼しげで若々しい色あい。ピンクを加えることがおしゃれっぽい。ヤングスポーツ。
3. 春の野原のような、のどかでソフトでさわやかさが感じられる。

1. 知性を感じさせる色あいに。グリーンを加えて若々しく。
2. 若々しく行動的な配色。紺で押えて大人ぽく。ヤングアダルト。
3. 類似色どうしの組み合わせ。鮮やかだが、やわらかいイメージ。

	C	M	Y	BL
	80	10	80	0
	0	5	100	0
	40	45	95	0

1

This is a smart color combination, with a touch of youthful green.

	C	M	Y	BL
	0	5	100	0
	100	65	0	0
	0	80	0	0

2

Here is a color scheme for the young and active. But with its mature sense of purple, this is also for young adults.

	C	M	Y	BL
	40	0	90	0
	0	5	100	0

3

A soft but bright image, composed of similar colors.

sexy modern セクシーモダン

		C	M	Y	BL
		0	0	60	0
		60	50	40	80

		C	M	Y	BL
		0	0	60	0
		60	50	40	80

LIGHT YELLOW

60 50 40 80

95 45 25 35

15 100 0 0

1

A combination of deep blue and pale yellow. Chic and tender.

2

A match of opposing colors, this combination awakens an adult sense of adventure and play.

1.深いブルーに淡いイエローを合わせて、シックで優しい感じ。

2.反対色の組み合わせ。大人の遊び心とか冒険心をくすぐるような感じ。

1. ペパーミントアイスクリームのようなさわ
   やかな色あい。
2. キャンディのようなファンタスティックで、
   可愛いい色あい。

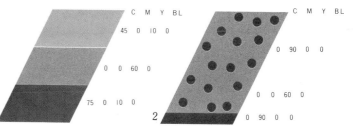

*A color match as fresh
as peppermint ice cream.*

*Fantastic and cute, like
candy.*

	C	M	Y	BL
	0	0	60	0
	35	5	60	0
	0	65	90	0

1

	C	M	Y	BL
	15	30	90	0
	55	70	0	0
	0	0	60	0

2

	C	M	Y	BL
	0	0	60	0
	100	0	60	0
	35	85	75	20

3

1. 軽快な配色が一層、若さをひきだしている。
2. ソフトな配色をベルトのオレンジがひきたてて、若々しさをだしている。
3. 淡い黄色とグリーンの配色を、ダークな赤がよりひきたてて、上品に。

A pleasant color scheme with a youthful spark.

A soft color arrangement, accented by the orange belt. Lots of youthful vitality.

A color scheme in pale yellow and green. The dark red gives it a sense of sophistication.

1. 反対色の組み合わせに、ビビッドなピンクを加えて、若々しく、生き生きした感じ。
2. 類似色の明度コントラスト。マイルドで、安心できる配色。
3. ライトトーンの配色。遊び心満点の楽しい配色。

1
A scheme using opposite colors, the vivid pink is youthful and alive.

2
Similar colors with a contrast of value. You can feel comfortable in these colors.

3
A light toned color arrangement. Full of fun.

C	M	Y	BL
0	0	60	0
55	70	0	0
0	100	15	0

C	M	Y	BL
0	0	60	0
45	55	75	40
35	45	95	0

C	M	Y	BL
90	5	10	0
0	0	60	0
100	0	60	0
0	80	0	0

	C	M	Y	BL
	65	70	0	0
	100	80	25	10
	0	25	80	0

1

	C	M	Y	BL
	0	25	80	0
	80	0	50	0

2

	C	M	Y	BL
	0	25	80	0
	20	80	20	20
	90	50	10	0

3

1.ハードな色使いだが、ノーブルな香りが漂よう
　よう。

2.さわやかな中に、ほのかな女っぽさが漂よう。

3.華やかな王侯貴族的なイメージ。ローズピ
　ンクが、ぜいたくなおしゃれ。

A bold use of color, with a touch of nobility.

Fresh and feminine, but modest.

A proud and aristocratic image. The rose pink gives it a sense of high fashion and luxury.

1. どこかノーブルな香りが漂う。クラシック。
2. ビビッドな色どうしの組み合わせ。明るく
   楽しく、生き生きとした感じ。

	C	M	Y	BL
	0	25	80	0
	45	45	75	50

	C	M	Y	BL
	0	70	95	0
	0	25	80	0

1 *A suggestion of nobility. Classic.*

2 *A vivid color arrangement. Bright, lively, and full of fun.*

	C	M	Y	BL
	0	25	80	0
	40	40	95	5
1	20	70	85	0

	C	M	Y	BL
	95	70	0	0
	60	0	5	0
2	0	25	80	0

1. アースカラーの組み合わせ。秋の気配が漂うよう。ソフトな感じ。
2. クールカラーにビビッドなイエローを加えて、知的な涼感。

An arrangement of earth colors. A soft sense of autumn.

Cool colors and vivid yellow, for a cool smart sense.

1. ビビッドな色どうしの配色にダークな茶を
   加えて、大人ぽく。ロック調。
2. 民族的色彩をモダン感覚でアレンジして楽しい。
3. 暖かみのある自然の色に、人工的な色を加
   えて、不思議なバランスをとっている。

	C	M	Y	BL
	0	25	80	0
	35	85	80	20
	0	100	70	0
1	0	45	95	0

	C	M	Y	BL
	0	25	80	0
	80	10	80	0
2	30	90	85	0

	C	M	Y	BL
	50	50	80	40
	100	70	25	10
	0	25	80	0
3	55	90	0	0

Vivid colors set off by dark brown. This is for adults who never forget those rock-'n'-rolls.

A fun folk-color arrangement with a modern sense.

The warmth of natural colors, mysteriously balanced with a touch of artificial color.

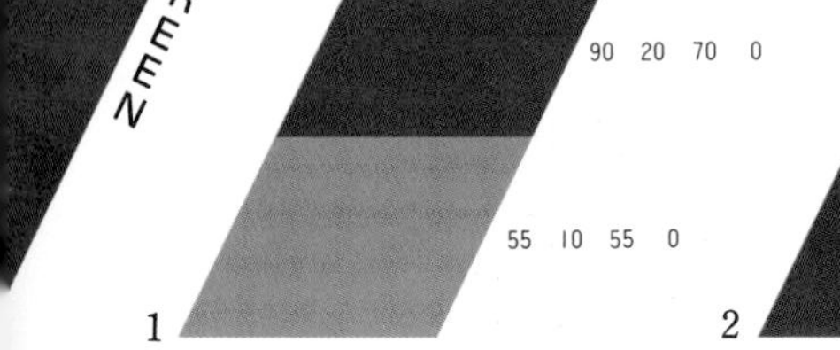

sexy modern セクシーモダン

GREEN

C M Y BL
90 20 70 0

55 10 55 0

1

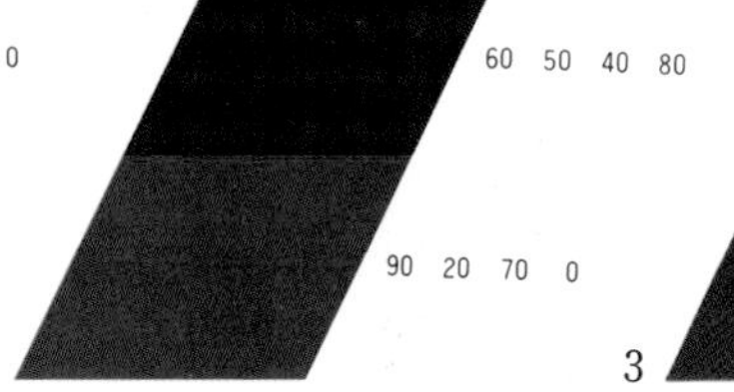

C M Y BL
60 50 40 80

90 20 70 0

2

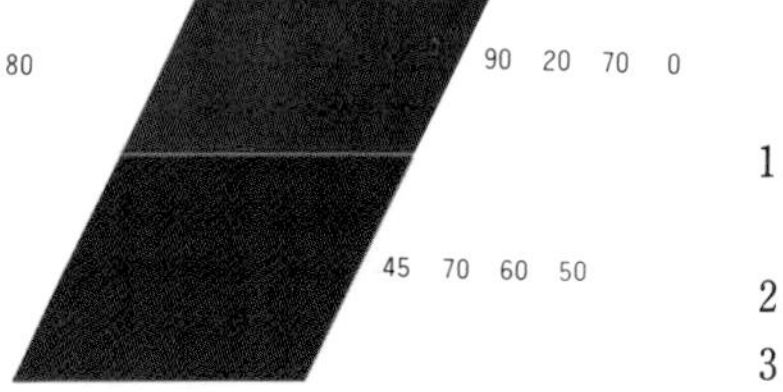

C M Y BL
90 20 70 0

45 70 60 50

3

1.ハードカラーも同系色の淡色で、ソフトに
イメージチェンジ。

2.ハード＆ハードだが、ノーブルなアダルト風。

3.ハードなマニッシュ感覚深みのある配色。

Hard colors can also become soft by image change through similar light colors.

"Hard & Hard" produces a noble adult feeling.

Hard mannish feeling with deep color schemes.

1.プリティカラーとダークカラーの意外な組み合わせが新鮮。

2.ダークトーンの面積が多く、ハードなイメージに大人ぽく。

3.ダイナミックな色相配色。ゴージャス。

	C	M	Y	BL
	0	25	5	0
	0	90	5	0
	90	20	70	0

1

	C	M	Y	BL
	15	50	0	0
	90	20	70	0

2

	C	M	Y	BL
	0	20	85	0
	90	20	70	0
	30	45	75	5

3

Unexpected color combination of pretty colors with dark colors can be refreshing.

When the area of dark tones is great, it produces a hard adult look.

Color scheme with dynamic hues is gorgeous.

	C	M	Y	BL
	90	20	70	0
	0	45	30	0
	15	35	65	0

	C	M	Y	BL
	70	30	45	5
	60	25	10	0
	90	20	70	0

	C	M	Y	BL
	90	20	70	0
	0	40	55	0
	90	30	35	40

1. An arrangement of strong and soft colors. Quiet and tranquil.

2. A strong contrast of red and green, tempered by gray.

3. Classic European high fashion.

1.ハード＆ソフトカラー配色。落ち着きがある。
2.グリーンに、赤の強いコントラストをグレーで中和させて……。
3.ダンディなヨーロッパ調、クラシック。

1.プリティカラーの軽さを、ディープカラー
　の面積でカバー。個性的に。

2.ライトカラーの面積が多く、若々しいスポー
　ティな配色。

3.グリーンの同系色の中に少量の赤を入れて、
　コントラストに効果。

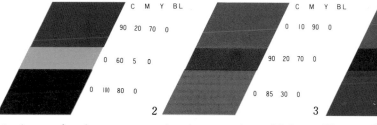

	C	M	Y	BL
	90	20	70	0
	0	60	5	0
	0	100	80	0

1

	C	M	Y	BL
	0	10	90	0
	90	20	70	0
	0	85	30	0

2

	C	M	Y	BL
	65	0	85	0
	95	0	50	0
	90	20	70	0

3

A deep color base, contrasted with pretty light colors. This arrangement has character.

A primary surface of light colors, this is a sporty and youthful arrangement.

The touch of red in this field of the juxtaposed greens makes an effective contrast.

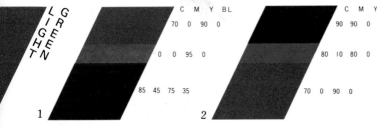

		C	M	Y	BL			C	M	Y	BL
		70	0	90	0			90	90	0	0
		0	0	95	0			80	10	80	0
		85	45	75	35			70	0	90	0

1 **2**

An arrangement of similar colors. A classic-modern friendly image.

A classic color arrangement with a hint of things to come. Also good for sportswear.

1. 類似色どうしの組み合わせ。クラシックモ
   ダンで優しいイメージ。
2. 古典的な配色だが、モダンな感覚も。スポー
   ツウェアの配合にも。

1.同色の濃淡を使って、ソフトで上品な感じ
　に。リボンの色でよりおしゃれ。
2.近い色どうしの組み合わせ。ロマンチック
　で華やかな感じ。

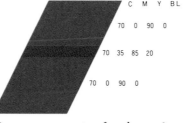

	C	M	Y	BL
	70	0	90	0
	70	35	85	20
	70	0	90	0

1

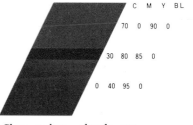

	C	M	Y	BL
	70	0	90	0
	30	80	85	0
	0	40	95	0

2

An arrangement of pale and opaque tones of the same color. Soft and refined, the color of the ribbon makes it fashionable.

Close colors, closely matched. Here is romance and luxury.

	C	M	Y	BL
	70	0	90	0
	40	25	15	0
	0	10	90	0
	40	65	80	30

1

	C	M	Y	BL
	0	90	65	0
	35	80	85	15
	70	0	90	0

2

	C	M	Y	BL
	70	0	90	0
	90	0	80	0
	100	80	0	0

3

1. 自然色の組み合わせ。心がなごむ配色にシルバーを加えて、少しゴージャス。

2. トロピカルな配色に茶色を加えて、一味大人ぽく。

3. 明るいグリーンに反対色の濃いブルーを加えて、都会的に。

1 *Natural colors in a comfortable mix, with a delightful touch of silver.*

2 *A tropical color arrangement, with a touch of brown. A bit of an adult mood.*

3 *Bright green, opposed by dark blue. For an urban look.*

1. 春の森、新芽の息吹きを感じさせる色あい
   にオレンジを加えてより明るく。
2. 夏のヨットハーバーを感じさせる。鮮やか
   な色あい。
3. トロピカルドリンクのような色。鮮やかな
   色どうしの組み合わせ。

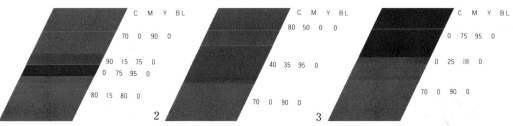

	C	M	Y	BL
	70	0	90	0
	90	15	75	0
	0	75	95	0
	80	15	80	0

1

	C	M	Y	BL
	80	50	0	0
	40	35	95	0
	70	0	90	0

2

	C	M	Y	BL
	0	75	95	0
	0	25	100	0
	70	0	90	0

3

The scent of fresh flowers in a spring forest. The touch of orange makes this color scheme even brighter.

These fresh colors make you think of boats in a summer harbor.

A fresh color arrangement. Like a tropical drink.

sexy modern セクシーモダン

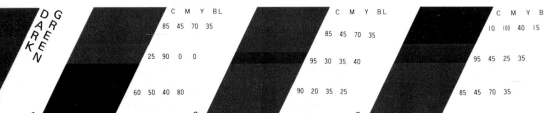

	C	M	Y	BL
DARKEN GREEN	85	45	70	35
	25	90	0	0
	60	50	40	80

1

	C	M	Y	BL
	85	45	70	35
	95	30	35	40
	90	20	35	25

2

	C	M	Y	BL
	10	100	40	15
	95	45	25	35
	85	45	70	35

3

Putting you in an autumn mood, chic and elegant.

Juxtaposed colors are arranged in contrasts of value. Modern, intelligent, feminine.

An classical arrangement of quiet hues.

1. 秋の気配を漂わせる、シックでエレガント
2. 明度差のある同系色どうしの組み合わせ。知的な女性ぽさがある。モダン。
3. 深味のある色あい。クラシック。

1. 反対色の使い方だが、色を渋く抑えてシックに。
2. 明度差のある同色系を使って、ソフトでナイーブに。

	C	M	Y	BL
	35	45	10	0
	45	45	0	0
	0	5	75	0
	85	45	70	35

	C	M	Y	BL
	0	0	60	0
	85	45	70	35

1 *Opposite colors, opaquely toned down for a chic look.*

2 *Juxtaposed colors, contrasted in value. Soft and sensitive.*

	C	M	Y	BL
	85	45	70	35
	25	45	75	0
	20	0	50	0
	45	45	80	30

1

Colors rich with the fragrance of the earth, contrasted in value.

	C	M	Y	BL
	95	0	50	0
	5	90	15	0
	65	70	20	10
	85	45	70	35

2

Bright and full of youth. Colors reminiscent of the folk traditions of the American Indian.

1. 大地の香りのするような色づかい。明度差をつけコントラスト。
2. 明るく、若々しい感じ。民族調、インディアンぽい色あい。

	C	M	Y	BL
	85	45	70	35
	0	30	80	0
	40	45	90	10

	C	M	Y	BL
	0	30	35	0
	15	20	90	0
	85	45	70	35

1.アメリカン・アーミー調、全体的に渋い感
　じだが、割と目立つ。

2.マニッシュな中に優しい、女らしさが漂っ
　ている。

1 *An American Army color scheme. Basically opaque, but eye-catching.*

2 *A bit boyish, but basically feminine and friendly.*

71

BLUE

	C	M	Y	BL
	95	10	0	0
	0	20	90	0
	85	95	20	0

1

It's easy to match similar colors. The yellow gives this noble mood a youth- ful quality.

	C	M	Y	BL
	95	10	0	0
	80	100	0	0
	20	100	0	10

2

Filled with the colors of adventure. The dark purple gives it an adult sense.

1. 類似色どうしはまとめやすい。ノーブルな
雰囲気にイエローが若々しい動きを加えている。
2. 冒険心いっぱいの色づかいに、ダークな紫
を加えて、アダルト感覚に。

72

1.明るい同系色どうしの組み合わせ。明るく、
　清潔で涼しい感じ。
2.明るく軽やかで涼しげな配色。ヤングカジ
　ュアル。

	C	M	Y	BL
	95	10	0	0
	75	15	75	0

	C	M	Y	BL
	30	80	5	5
	95	10	0	0

1 *Bright, cool, and clean. An arrangement of juxta-posed bright colors.*

2 *Bright, cool, and light. A young, casual look.*

	C	M	Y	BL
	95	10	0	0
	10	100	40	15
	30	90	70	15

1

	C	M	Y	BL
	0	70	30	0
	10	40	70	0
	95	10	0	0

2

	C	M	Y	BL
	95	10	0	0
	0	35	65	0
	40	60	85	20

3

1.色相のコントラスト。海に沈む夕日のイメージ。

2.軽やかで、健康的なヤングカジュアル。

3.反対色の組み合わせ。さえわたる空と大地のイメージ。

A contrast of color, like the sun setting on the ocean.

Light and healthy, for a young casual look.

An arrangement of color opposites. Like the earth and the clear blue sky.

1. 反対色の組み合わせ。スポーティで、パンチ力もある。
2. 春のイメージ。クールカラーを使っているが、冷めたさを感じさせない。
3. 鮮やかな色のトレイド配色。ウキウキするような遊び心。スポーティ、スキーウェアにも。

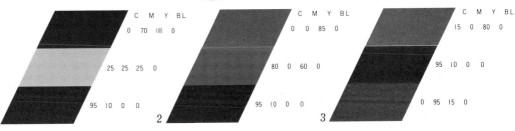

	C	M	Y	BL
	0	70	100	0
	25	25	25	0
	95	10	0	0

1 *Contrast color combination. Sporty as well as bold.*

	C	M	Y	BL
	0	0	85	0
	80	0	60	0
	95	10	0	0

2 *Images of spring. Although using cool colors, there is no cold feeling.*

	C	M	Y	BL
	15	0	80	0
	95	10	0	0
	0	95	15	0

3 *A color scheme of vivid colors. For the lively, funloving soul. Appropriate for sporty ski wear.*

			C M Y BL			C M Y BL
			75 15 0 0			75 15 0 0
			90 25 45 30			30 85 25 40
			55 15 40 0			75 55 0 0

LIGHT BLUE

1.淡い色調にダークなグリーンを加えて、大
人ぽい、優しい感じ。

2.同系色でまとめて、紫陽花のように、しっ
とりとして、知的で涼しげな感じ。

1
Adding dark green to light colors produces a mature soothing feeling.

2
Combination of juxtaposed color tones. Like the hydrangea on the left it produces mental serenity.

1.優しく、やわらかい、春のイメージ。ロマンチック。
2.ノーマルな配色にビビッドなピンクがアクセント。可愛らしい、お嬢さんカラー。
3.同系色でまとめやすい後退色。柔らかいが、どこか冷たい感じのする色あい。

	C	M	Y	BL
1	75	15	0	0
	60	0	30	0

	C	M	Y	BL
2	0	60	10	0
	0	95	25	0
	75	15	0	0

	C	M	Y	BL
3	85	60	0	0
	75	15	0	0

The images of spring-soft, merrow and romantic.

Vivid pink is used to accent normal color scheme. A cute young miss' color.

Receding colors easy to combine with juxtaposed colors. Soft but with tones producing a cold feeling.

	C	M	Y	BL
	70	15	0	0
	80	35	15	5
	75	15	75	0

1

	C	M	Y	BL
	15	90	90	0
	85	45	70	30
	70	15	0	0

2

	C	M	Y	BL
	70	15	0	0
	95	45	0	0
	90	30	25	40

3

Refreshing outdoor colors. Adding gray produces a calm effect.

Like a setting sun into the sea. Using contrast colors.

Juxtaposed tone portraying the mysterious colors of the sea.

1.アウトドアーカラーで爽やか、グレーを加えて、落ち着かせて。

2.海に沈む夕日の感じ。反対色を使って。

3.神秘的な海の色を同系色で。

1.明るいブルーに同明度のグレーを加えて、
　知的な感じに。インテリア小物にも。

2.明るいブルーに同明度のイエローをポイン
　トにして、すっきりとし行動的に。

3.明るい色どうしの組み合わせ。プリティカ
　ラーを、スポーティ感覚に。

	C	M	Y	BL
	30	15	0	0
	80	35	15	5
1	70	15	0	0

	C	M	Y	BL
	0	5	90	0
	70	15	0	0
2				

	C	M	Y	BL
	70	15	0	0
	5	70	5	0
3				

The same value of gray is added to bright blue to produce an intellectual effect. Suitable for small interior goods.

Using similar bright values of yellow with bright blue is an accentuating point. Fresh and live with action.

Color combination with vivid colors. Pretty colors brought together for a sporty feeling.

	C M Y BL		C M Y BL
DARK BLUE	90 25 45 30		85 95 20 0
	0 100 15 0		95 0 50 0
	100 80 0 0		90 25 45 30

1 *Among juxtaposed colors of blue adding vivid pink gives a dressy look.*

2 *Color combination of rich aristocratic colors. High class feeling and haute couture.*

1.同系色のブルーの中に、ビビッドなピンクを加えておしゃれぽく。

2.貴族的な色の組み合わせ。高級感、オートクチュール。

1. フランスの貴族の子女のイメージ。メルヘンティック。
2. 同系色どうしの組み合わせ。ロマンチックな品のよさ。
3. 落ち着いた配色。透んだ星空のイメージ。知的なアダルト感覚。

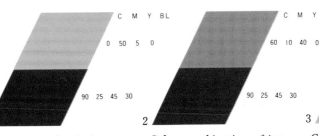

	C	M	Y	BL
	0	50	5	0
1	90	25	45	30

	C	M	Y	BL
	60	10	40	0
2	90	25	45	30

	C	M	Y	BL
	90	25	45	30
3	35	40	0	0

1 *The image of a little miss from a noble French family.*

2 *Color combination of juxtaposed colors. For romantic items.*

3 *Calm, serene color scheme. Transparent like a starry night. Sophisticated adult look.*

	C	M	Y	BL
	20	35	60	0
	0	40	10	0
	90	25	45	30

1

	C	M	Y	BL
	90	25	45	30
	50	45	95	5
	40	35	30	40

2

Value contrast balance well. Produces a subtle, charming and youthful look.

Color combination with intermediate color value. Serene, quiet mood giving the sensation of largeness.

1. 明度対比がバランスよく、優しさ、甘さ、若々しさをかもしだしている。
2. 中明度どうしの組み合わせ。落ち着いたムード、静寂、大きさを感じさせる。

1. 人工的で寂しい感じを与えるが、ビビッド
   なピンクがアクセント。
2. 安心感を与える配色。濃淡の組み合わせが
   個性的。
3. 可愛らしさの中に少し大人ぽさを感じる。
   ピンクがきれいに見える。

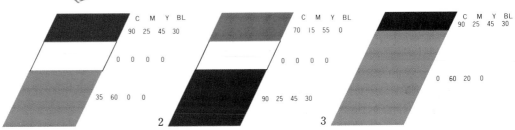

	C	M	Y	BL
1	90	25	45	30
	0	0	0	0
	35	60	0	0

	C	M	Y	BL
2	70	15	55	0
	0	0	0	0
	90	25	45	30

	C	M	Y	BL
3	90	25	45	30
	0	60	20	0

1   *Gives the feeling of artificial lonliness however with vivid pink accents.*

2   *Color schemes giving the feeling of safeness. Combination of shades produces individuality.*

3   *While cute, it is a little grown-up. The pink appears charmingly pleasing.*

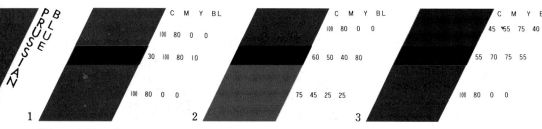

			C	M	Y	BL
			100	80	0	0
			30	100	80	10
			100	80	0	0
1						

		C	M	Y	BL
		100	80	0	0
		60	50	40	80
		75	45	25	25
2					

		C	M	Y	BL
		45	55	75	40
		55	70	75	55
		100	80	0	0
3					

PRUSSIAN BLUE

1. ダークカラーにビビッドな色をポイントに使い、個性的。

2. ダークトーン配色なので、ライトカラーを入れて効果的に。

3. 茶系を紺でスマートにまとめ、ソフィスケートなアダルトイメージ。

1 Using vivid colors against dark colors is a point here. Individualistic.

2 A dark color scheme incorporating light colors is effective.

3 Combining browns with dark blue produces stylish look, a sophisticated adult image.

1. クールカラー（寒色）どうしのクリアな組み合わせ。
2. 同系色どうしは、ハーモニーがとれやすい。ブルーでまとめて清楚な感じ。
3. シャープな紺とソフトなベージュは、うまくマッチする。

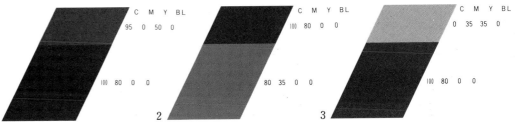

1　*Cool colors (cold colors) produce clear combinations.*

2　*Easy to harmonize the juxtaposed colors. A combination of blues produce a neat and trim feeling.*

3　*Sharp dark blue and soft beige coordinates well.*

	C	M	Y	BL
	100	80	0	0
	70	50	15	5
	20	95	70	5

1

Orthodox dark color s-cheme. Youthful but classic.

	C	M	Y	BL
	100	80	0	0
	0	100	0	0
	95	50	15	0

2

A youthful color combination with the accent point of using pink with colors similar to blues.

	C	M	Y	BL
	100	80	0	0
	40	15	40	0
	90	35	60	25

3

Sober and hard dark blue combination with green shade.

1. オーソドックスなダークカラーの配色。ヤングクラシック。
2. ブルーの類似色に、ピンクをポイントにした若々しい組み合わせ。
3. グリーンの濃淡と、紺の地味でハードな組み合わせ。

1. ベージュと紺のニュートラルな組み合わせ。シンプルでモダンな感じ。
2. クリアなイエローがベースなので、ダークカラーと合わせても若々しい。
3. 単調になりがちなパステルカラーの組み合わせも、紺でぐっと引きしまる。

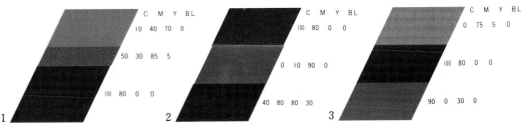

	C	M	Y	BL
	10	40	70	0
	50	30	85	5
	100	80	0	0

1 *Beige and dark blue produce a neutral color combination. Simple and modern.*

	C	M	Y	BL
	100	80	0	0
	0	10	90	0
	40	80	80	30

2 *Clear yellow as a base combined with dark colors produces a young feeling, as well.*

	C	M	Y	BL
	0	75	5	0
	100	80	0	0
	90	0	30	0

3 *Color combinations of pastel colors are sometimes monotonous, however, the dark blue gives it tightness.*

		C M Y BL			C M Y BL

GRAYISH BLUE

85 50 20 10

0 0 60 0

65 60 0 0

90 75 30 20

45 35 40 50

25 50 75 0

85 50 20 10

1

Adding differing value and hues of yellow to blues produces an active young feeling.

2

Tones that subdue colors have warmth. Produce classic mood.

1.同系色のブルーに、明度差、色相差のある
　イエローを加えて、行動的で若々しく。

2.全体的に色味を抑えた色あいだが、暖かみ
　のある、クラシックムードをだしている。

1.同系色で合わせやすい。エレガンスムード。
2.寒色系の組み合わせ。夢見るようなロマンチックムード。

	C	M	Y	BL
	5	70	0	0
	85	50	20	10

	C	M	Y	BL
	85	50	20	10
	95	10	40	0

1

2

Easy to combine juxtaposed colors. Elegant mood.

Color combinations with cold colors. Dreamy romantic mood.

	C	M	Y	BL
	40	30	15	0
	15	20	90	0
	15	90	90	0
	85	50	20	10

	C	M	Y	BL
	85	50	20	10
	0	40	10	0
	95	45	0	0
	20	35	60	0

1
Gray is used as a plus in medium-valued color schemes. Produces a playful mood.

2
Value contrast. Pink produces a sweet, young feeling.

1.中明度のトレイド配色にグレーをプラスして、遊び心を出している。

2.明度コントラスト。ピンクが全体を甘い若々しい感じにしている。

1. 淡いブルーに、ビビッドな色を加えて、ウ
   キウキする遊び心充分。
2. 寒色系でまとめて、ちょっとマニッシュな
   感覚に。ヤングカジュアル。

	C	M	Y	BL
	0	75	0	0
	85	50	20	10
1	95	0	40	0

	C	M	Y	BL
	65	15	80	0
	85	0	40	0
2	85	50	20	10

*By adding vivid colors to
light blue is enough to
produce a lively, fun-lov-
ing feeling.*

*Combinations of cold colors.
Slightly mannish feeling. For
casual.*

sexy modern セクシーモダン

Sonorous adult feeling. Dignified and mysterious mood.

Value contrast. Classic and elegant.

	C	M	Y	BL
	10	90	0	0
	85	50	35	40

	C	M	Y	BL
	90	25	45	30
	10	0	85	0
	85	50	35	40

DEEP BLUE

1

2

1. 格調高いアダルト感覚。高貴で神秘的なムード。

2. 明度コントラスト。クラシックでエレガンス。

1. 寒色系の組み合わせに、ピンクをアクセントとして、明るくソフトに。
2. 明度コントラスト。エレガントで高貴な雰囲気。

	C	M	Y	BL
	30	0	0	0
	80	0	35	0
	0	70	15	0
	85	50	35	40

	C	M	Y	BL
	100	25	0	0
	85	50	35	40

1

Accenting with pink in cold color combinations produces a brighter and softer look.

2

Value contrast. Elegant and dignified atmosphere.

	C	M	Y	BL
	85	50	35	40
	45	40	45	60
	95	45	0	0

1

	C	M	Y	BL
	15	85	20	10
	95	0	60	0
	85	50	35	40

2

	C	M	Y	BL
	60	35	85	5
	85	50	35	40

3

1. 明度コントラストが絶妙。シンプルでシック
2. ライトトーンを紺で抑えて、シックな感覚に。着物にも使われる色あい。
3. 全体に渋い色調で、ナイーブな感じ。

The value contrast is superb. Simple and chic.

Light tones subdued by dark blue produce chic feeling. Colors also used for kimono.

Overall elegant, sober color tones. Naïve feeling.

1. ビビッドな色を紺で抑えて、リゾート感覚で若々しく。
2. 暖かみのあるアースカラーを紺でひきしめて。（オーストラリアの台地のイメージ）
3. 秋の気配が漂う色づかい。

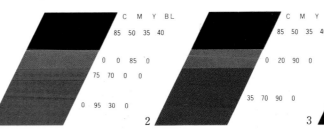

	C	M	Y	BL
1	85	50	35	40
	0	0	85	0
	75	70	0	0
	0	95	30	0

	C	M	Y	BL
2	85	50	35	40
	0	20	90	0
	35	70	90	0

	C	M	Y	BL
3	20	25	90	0
	65	15	80	0
	40	60	85	20
	85	50	35	40

1 *Vivid colors subdued by dark blue. Young with feeling of resorts.*

2 *Warm earth-color combination with a tight deep blue. (images of color resembling the Australian tableland)*

3 *Colors suggesting the mood of autumn.*

95

VIOLET

	C M Y BL		C M Y BL
	60 70 15 10		60 70 15 10
1 25 90 70 20		**2** 90 35 70 5	

Classic. Image of a serene
mature person.

Gorgeous color schemes
using deep colors.

1. クラシックで落ち着いた大人のイメージ。
2. ディープカラーどうしのゴージャスな配色。

1. 女性ぽくソフトなロマンチックカラー。
2. 類似色どうしのデリケートなニュアンスの
　　ある配色。

	C	M	Y	BL
	0	40	10	0
	60	70	15	10

	C	M	Y	BL
	60	70	15	10
	70	50	15	5

1 *Feminine and soft romantic color.*

2 *Color tones with the delicate nuance of affinitive colors.*

		C	M	Y	BL
	1	75	35	10	0
		60	70	15	10

		C	M	Y	BL
	2	60	70	15	10
		95	25	0	0
		100	70	25	10

		C	M	Y	BL
	3	70	20	35	0
		60	70	15	10

1.ナイーヴで中性的配色。
2.ナチュラルな類似色でシックなイメージ。
3.中間色どうしの粋な組み合わせ。

1
Naïve, neutral tones.

2
Chic image with natural affinitive colors.

3
Stylish combinations with intermediate colors.

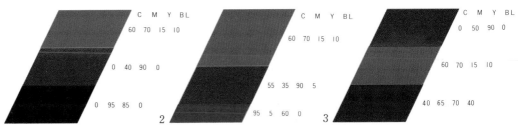

1. イエローと紫の色相対比に赤を加えて、よりビビッドに。
2. 反対色の組み合わせ。大胆だけどそれなりにマッチする。
3. ナチュラルに調和しあった健康的な配色。アダルトイメージ。

	C	M	Y	BL
	60	70	15	10
	0	40	90	0
1	0	95	85	0

	C	M	Y	BL
	60	70	15	10
	55	35	90	5
2	95	5	60	0

	C	M	Y	BL
	0	50	90	0
	60	70	15	10
3	40	65	70	40

Red added to the yellow and violet color contrast makes it more vivid.

Combinations with contrast colors. Bold but matching.

A healthy looking color schme harmonized naturally. Adult image.

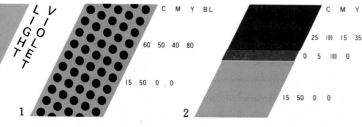

CMYBL

60 50 40 80

15 50 0 0

1

Adding black to light violet produces individualistic elegance.

CMYBL

25 100 15 35

0 5 100 0

15 50 0 0

2

Juxtaposed colors differing in value. Accent with contrasting yellow. Chic, noble feeling.

LIGHT VIOLET

1.淡い紫に黒を加えて、個性的なエレガンス。
2.明度差のある同系色。反対色の黄色をアクセントに。シックでノーブルな感じ。

1.同系色どうしの組み合わせ、しっとりした
　やわらかさ。
2.淡く、透明感のある色調を、紺でぐっと引
　き締めて。

	C	M	Y	BL
	15	50	0	0
	20	80	20	20

	C	M	Y	BL
	0	20	35	0
	95	65	20	15
	60	50	40	80
	15	50	0	0

1 *Combination with juxtaposed colors. Gentle softness.*

2 *Light, transparent color tones are drawn in by dark blue.*

	C	M	Y	BL
	15	50	0	0
	65	60	0	0
1	100	85	0	0

	C	M	Y	BL
	35	80	25	15
	15	50	0	0
2	45	60	70	55

	C	M	Y	BL
	25	10	60	0
	75	30	70	0
3	15	50	0	0

1. 類似配色が優雅な雰囲気をだしている。
2. 明度、彩度を抑えた赤で統一したアダルトな感覚。
3. 反対色を淡くまとめて、静かで落ち着いた雰囲気に。

1 *Color schemes with affinitive colors produce a graceful atmosphere.*

2 *Adult image unified by red which subdues the value and chroma.*

3 *Contrast colors are lightly combined. Serene tranquil atmosphere.*

1. 反対色どうしを淡い色調でまとめて、春の風に揺れるやさしい花のイメージ。
2. 明度コントラストの配色が、楽しい花園を思わせる。
3. どことなく人工的で冷たい感じがする。清潔感もでている。

	C	M	Y	BL
	30	0	45	0
	95	15	25	20
	15	50	0	0

	C	M	Y	BL
	15	50	0	0
	20	80	75	0

	C	M	Y	BL
	60	0	20	0
	85	20	45	5
	15	50	0	0

1 *Contrast colors are combined in light tones. Image of graceful flowers swaying in the spring breeze.*

2 *Color tones of value contrasts remind us of a colorful flower garden.*

3 *Somehow artificial with a sense of coldness. It has a neat, clean feeling.*

DARK VIOLET

	C	M	Y	BL
	70	95	10	10
	95	45	25	35

1

Combination of sonorous adult colors—Dandy.

	C	M	Y	BL
	70	95	10	10
	45	35	40	50

2

Classic, refined serenity. Also displays a cool feeling.

	C	M	Y	BL
	100	60	5	0
	70	95	10	10

3

Heavy colors used emphasize feminity.

1.格調高いアダルトカラーの組み合わせで、ダンディぱく。

2.クラシックで上品な落ち着き。涼感もある。

3.重量感のある色づかいが女性らしさを強調している。

1. トーン・オン・トーンの優雅さが、和服の
   配色を思わせる。
2. 柔らか味のある色あい。明るいグリーンを
   アクセントに。優雅な感じ。

	C	M	Y	BL
	0	50	0	0
	0	75	0	0
	70	95	10	10

1

	C	M	Y	BL
	70	95	10	10
	75	50	15	0

2

Gracefulness of tone-on-tone reminds one of in kimono.

Color schemes with a softness. Bright green used as an accent providing exquisite richness.

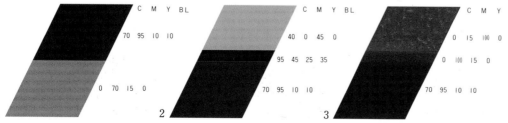

	C	M	Y	BL
	70	95	10	10
	0	70	15	0

1

Effect of value contrast. Soft mood while at the same time adult-like and child-like.

	C	M	Y	BL
	40	0	45	0
	95	45	25	35
	70	95	10	10

2

The combination of contrast colors is drawn in by dark blue producing elegance.

	C	M	Y	BL
	0	15	100	0
	0	100	15	0
	70	95	10	10

3

The contrasting violet and yellow are balanced by an intermediate red. Like a carnival.

1.明度のコントラスト効果。ソフトなムードで大人のような、少女のような。

2.反対色の組み合わせを紺で引き締めて、エレガントに。

3.紫と反対色の黄色を、中間の赤でバランスをとって、カーニバル的色あい。

1. 大胆な色の使い方。妙にマッチして春の野
   原の感じ。
2. 若々しいが心が落ち着く色あい。ヤングア
   ダルト。
3. 紫の濃淡に明るい反対色のグリーンを入れ
   て若々しく、スポーティでエレガント。

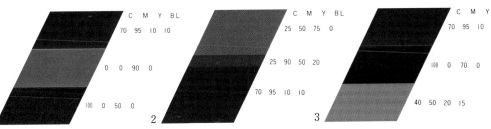

	C	M	Y	BL
	70	95	10	10
	0	0	90	0
	100	0	50	0

1

	C	M	Y	BL
	25	50	75	0
	25	90	50	20
	70	95	10	10

2

	C	M	Y	BL
	70	95	10	10
	100	0	70	0
	40	50	20	15

3

Using bold colors. Surprisingly when matched, stirs up thoughts of a spring filed.

A color schme which is young looking while tranquil. Young adult.

Bright contrasting green is added to shades of violet giving a young feeling. Sporty while elegant.

107

1.ディープトーンの強烈な配色が、ワイルド
　な感覚をだしている。
2.強烈な配色の中に、上品さがでている。個
　性派感覚。

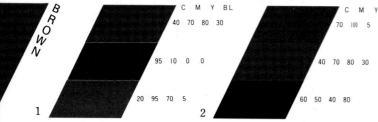

	C	M	Y	BL
	40	70	80	30
	95	10	0	0
	20	95	70	5

	C	M	Y	BL
	70	100	5	5
	40	70	80	30
	60	50	40	80

BROWN

1
The deep tones of dazzling color schemes produce a wild feeling.

2
Within the dazzling color schemes there is a refined elegance. Individualistic feeling.

1. ウォームカラーでまとめてソフトに。アメ
   リカウェスタンのイメージ。
2. 反対色の組み合わせだが、深みのある色を
   重ねて、重量感を出している。クラシック。

	C	M	Y	BL
	45	45	80	30
	0	0	40	0
	40	70	80	30

	C	M	Y	BL
	40	70	80	30
	90	25	45	30

1

The combined warm colors produce a softness. Image of Americana.

2

Combined contrast colors overlapping deep colors produces a heaviness. Classic.

	C	M	Y	BL
	40	65	70	40
	0	20	35	0
	40	70	80	30

1

Juxtaposed colors combined together produces a soft, sweet harmonious effect.

	C	M	Y	BL
	40	70	80	30
	0	50	95	0
	65	25	90	0

2

Green distributed over affinitive browns produces a folklore tone.

	C	M	Y	BL
	0	100	65	0
	60	50	40	80
	40	70	80	30

3

Adding black to juxtaposed colors makes it passionate. Spanish tone.

1.同系色でまとめて、ソフトで甘いハーモニーをかもしだしている。

2.茶の類似色にグリーンを配して、フォークロア、民族調に。

3.同系色に黒をプラスして、情熱的に。スペイン調。

1. 茶に淡いブルーを加えて、さわやかでナイーブな感じ。
2. 明るい同系色でまとめて、軽快で明るい感じ。アメリカ娘のように。

	C	M	Y	BL
	40	5	5	0
	0	20	35	0
	40	70	80	30

	C	M	Y	BL
	0	65	90	0
	0	100	65	0
	40	70	80	30

1 *Adding light blue to brown produces a fresh naïve feeling.*

2 *Combined with bright juxtaposed colors, it produces a light gay feeling. Like an American girl.*

			C	M	Y	BL
			20	40	40	0
			10	40	70	0
1			35	70	85	5

	C	M	Y	BL
	40	45	0	5
2	35	70	85	5

	C	M	Y	BL
	35	70	85	5
	90	0	70	0
3	45	60	70	60

LIGHT BROWN

Subdue contrast to pro-duce elegant color image.

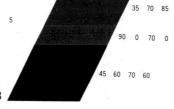

To give the feeling of autumn—a noble, warm color scheme.

Distributing soft green on browns produces a mature woman's image.

1. コントラストを抑えて、エレガントなカラー
   イメージ。
2. 秋を思わせる、ノーブルで温かい配色。
3. 茶の同系色にソフトなグリーンを配して、
   ハイミセスのイメージ。

1. 開放的なセパレーション効果。
2. 南国エスニック調。大胆で個性的。
3. ノーブルな秋配色、黒がひきしめ役。

	C	M	Y	BL
1		35	70	85	5
	100	80	0	0
	100	50	0	0

Open separation-effect.

	C	M	Y	BL
2		35	70	85	5
	0	95	20	0
	80	35	90	0

Southern countries' ethnic tone. Bold, individualistic.

	C	M	Y	BL
3		15	95	85	0
	60	50	40	80
	35	70	85	5

Noble autumn color scheme where the black draws the scheme together.

	C	M	Y	BL
	35	70	85	5
	60	0	35	0
1	30	60	85	0

	C	M	Y	BL
	0	25	90	0
	30	45	75	0
2	35	70	85	5

	C	M	Y	BL
	35	70	85	5
	35	70	60	30
3	45	45	80	30

The brown is accented with green. Produces a slightly charming mannish feeling.

Color combination frequently used for resort wear.

Wild color schemes of earth colors.

1. 茶系にグリーンをアクセントにした、少し甘いマニッシュ感覚。
2. リゾートウェアによく使われるファッションカラー。
3. アースカラーどうしのワイルドな配色。

1.なじみやすいナチュラルな組み合わせ。
2.スポーティな中にも落ち着きがある。ダンディ。
3.ソフトなウォームカラーの組み合わせ。

	C	M	Y	BL
1	35	70	85	5
	60	25	90	0
	0	65	90	0
	0	0	40	0

Easy to adapt natural color scheme.

	C	M	Y	BL
2	35	70	85	5
	95	45	0	0
	90	0	0	0
	0	0	0	0

One of the quieter ones among the sporty look. Dandy.

	C	M	Y	BL
3	0	25	90	0
	40	100	50	0
	35	70	85	5

Color scheme of soft, warm colors.

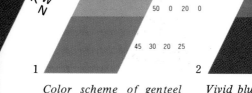

	C M Y BL		C M Y BL		C M Y BL
DARK BROWN	40 50 60 45		95 20 15 0		40 50 60 45
	50 0 20 0		65 55 0 0		0 0 50 0
	45 30 20 25		40 50 60 45		85 40 70 30
1		**2**		**3**	

1.上品な茶とグレーの配色に、淡いグリーン
を加えてノーブルに。

2.ダークな配色に、ビビッドなブルーを配し
て個性的に。ヨーロッパ調。

3.メンズカラーに、淡いイエローを加えて、
ソフトに。

1
Color scheme of genteel brown and gray with the addition of light green to produce a nobleness.

2
Vivid blue distributed over dark color schemes produces an individualistic look. European tone.

3
Adding light yellow to men's color to produce a soft look.

1.明度コントラスト。ソフトで可愛いい感じ。
　プリント柄によってはソフトにもハードにも。
2.ソフトで甘いウォームカラーの組み合わせ。
　ロマンチック。

	C	M	Y	BL
	0	0	95	0
1	40	50	60	45

	C	M	Y	BL
	0	60	90	0
	15	40	50	0
2	40	50	60	45

Value contrast. Soft and cute. Can be soft or hard depending on the print design.

Combining soft, sweet warm colors. Romantic.

	C	M	Y	BL
	40	50	60	45
	30	0	35	0
	40	35	90	5

1
Warm feeling. Mannish color scheme.

	C	M	Y	BL
	0	0	40	0
	30	50	80	0
	40	50	60	45

2
Like warm sunshine.

	C	M	Y	BL
	40	50	60	45
	0	5	75	0
	0	75	35	0

3
Warm color combination like an autumn sun shining brilliantly.

1．ぬくもりの感じられる、マニッシュな配色。
2．ほのぼのとした日だまりを思わせる、暖かい色あい。
3．秋の日に明るく輝やく感じ。ウォームカラーの組み合わせ。

1. 秋の淋しさの中に若さと甘ずっぱさを感じ
させる。ロマンチック。
2. 配色しやすい色。秋の気配、秋の空と落葉
を感じさせる。
3. 茶の同系色にソフトなグリーンを加えて、
心もなごむ。おおらかな感じ。

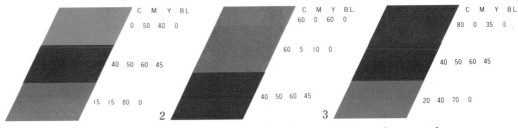

	C	M	Y	BL
1	0	50	40	0
	40	50	60	45
	15	15	80	0

	C	M	Y	BL
2	60	0	60	0
	60	5	10	0
	40	50	60	45

	C	M	Y	BL
3	80	0	35	0
	40	50	60	45
	20	40	70	0

Produces the sensation of youth, and sweet & sour within the loneliness of autumn. Romantic.

Easy color to use in color scheme. Provides the mood of autumn with the autumn sky and fallen leaves.

Adding soft green to brown produces a soothing effect. Magnanimous sensation.

カラーイメージII　COLOR IMAGE II

●パステルカラー

ロマンティック、フェミニン、メルヘンティック、甘美な、やさしいなど全体的に柔らかい感じの言葉で表現される色。夢のあるやさしいイメージなので、春先の華やかさにコーディネートされる色になりやすい。
（レース、花柄、春）

●ビビッドカラー

鮮やかで、はっきりした色なので、白を生かすことができます。活動的な感じなので、カジュアルやスポーティなものに合うでしょう。
（遊園地、ネオン）

●グレイッシュカラー

シックで気品があり落ち着いた色。自然色であるので情緒が感じられ、一般的に地味になりやすいが、無難な感じでコーディネートしやすい。（土、陶器、苔）

●ダークカラー

ダンディさとハードな雰囲気で安定した感じがあるので、男性用品の主流になっている。ダーク色は、深みがあるので格調が感じられる。（アンティーク家具、革用品）

●モノトーン

他の色をアクセントとしてきかせることができ、白は清潔感があり他の色をひきたてて美しく見せます。グレーは穏やかな感じで、モノトーンとの組み合わせでは和らげる働きをします。黒は大人ぽくベーシックなイメージ。
（イブニングドレス、高級車）

● Pastel Colors

Overall, the soft fluffy images of Pastel Colors can be expressed as romantic, feminine, Cinderella-like or sugary-sweet. With such dream-like imaginary they are colors that can be easily coordinated with the beauty of early spring. (Lace, Flower Vases, Spring)

● Vivid Colors

As these colors are vivid and clear, they bring out the purity of white. Radiating the feeling of action, they are suitable for casual and sports wear. (Amusement Parks, Neon Lights)

● Grayish Colors

Chic, these colors portray a serene, refine quality. Being natural colors there are strong deep emotions associated with them. Although they have a tendency to become dull, they can be safely coordinated with a sense of security. (Earth, Pottery, Moss)

● Dark Colors

Being dandy while stable colors, they project a hard look and are the mainstream of men's products. Because there is depth in them, they have a style within them. (Antique Furniture, Leather Goods)

● Monotone

These monotones can be used to accentuate other colors. White has a clean appearance that enhances other colors setting them off beautifully. Gray has a pacifying effect which works as a neutralizer. As for black, it has a basic image of maturity. (Evening Dress, Luxury Cars)

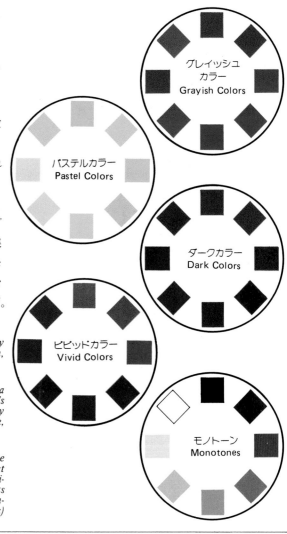

グレイッシュカラー　Grayish Colors
パステルカラー　Pastel Colors
ダークカラー　Dark Colors
ビビッドカラー　Vivid Colors
モノトーン　Monotones

パステル＋ビビッド

明度の高い色と彩度の高い色との組み合わせなので、パーッと明るく目立つ印象を与えるが、パステルカラーがビビッドカラーの強さを和らげてくれるので、嫌味のない、好感の持てる明るさが得られる。

Pastel + Vivid

When a color with high value and a color with high chroma are combined, they imprint a striking, eye-catching impression on the mind. As the Pastel Color softens the intensity of the Vivid Color, a pleasant type of brightness without any negative aftereffects is obtained.

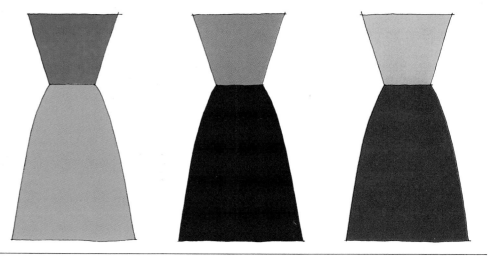

パステル＋ダーク

明るさと暗さの配色で、比較的無難にまとめやすい。パステルカラーの色みを彩やかにすると聡明な感じになり、逆に色みを抑えるとシックでおしゃれっぽい印象を与える。

Pastel + Dark

A color scheme employing bright and dark colors can be coordinated with relatively a sense of security. When the tint of Pastel Colors is colorfully applied, an intellectual effect is achieved, while contrastingly, when the tint is suppressed, a chic, stylish image is projected.

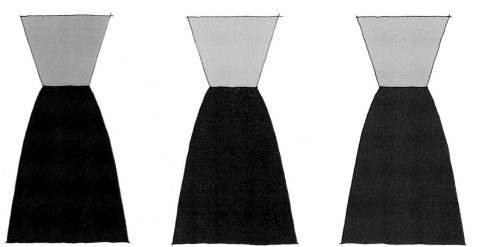

パステル＋グレイッシュ

不透明でぼけた色どうしの組み合わせだが、パステルカラーの色みを彩やかにすることでさわやかな明るさになる。逆に色みを抑えてしまうと落ち着き過ぎてしまい、消極的で若さに欠けた配色にもなりうる。

Pastel + Grayish

When the tint of a Pastel Color is colorfully applied in a color scheme with both colors being opaque and gradated, a fresh kind of brightness is achieved. Conversely, when the tint is suppressed, it becomes too sober with the color scheme lacking in youthfulness.

ビビッド＋ダーク

彩度・明度の低いダークカラーが、彩やかなビビッドカラーを自然と浮きあがらせて、しっかりと引き立て役にまわるといった組み合わせ。分量的にはダークカラーに対して、ビビッドカラーを少しポイント的に持ってくると、効果的な配色になる。

Vivid + Dark

Dark colors with low chroma and color value naturally set off colorful Vivid Colors and in color schemes they have an effect that strongly enhances. If Dark Colors are quantitatively used to slightly accentuate Vivid Colors, an effective color scheme can be achieved.

ビビッド＋グレイッシュ

透明と不透明のコントラスト配色。ビビッド＋ダークの組み合わせと同じく、グレイッシュがビビッドの引き立て役になるが、ビビッド＋ダークの組み合わせに比べると、グレイッシュカラーの効果で、きつさが和らげられて、女らしいイメージになる。

Vivid + Grayish

This is a transparent-opaque contrast color scheme. Similar to color schemes employing Vivid and Dark Colors, Grayish Colors act as an enhancer of Vivid Colors. In comparison to Vivid + Dark color schemes, the harshness is moderated from the effect of the Grayish Color projecting a feminine image.

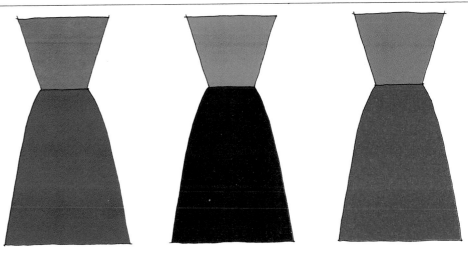

ダーク＋グレイッシュ

コクの深さと渋さの組み合わせ。ダークカラーはコクがあり、透明感のある色ではあるが、緊張感を伴うので、印象的にきつさがある。それをグレイッシュカラーの鈍さで和らげると、ぐっと大人っぽい感じになる。

Dark + Grayish

This is a color scheme combining deep overtones and soberness. Dark Colors have a depth within them and along with the tense feeling of transparent colors there is an impressionable harshness. The Dark Colors moderate the sharpness of Grayish Colors giving off a very sophisticated mature look.

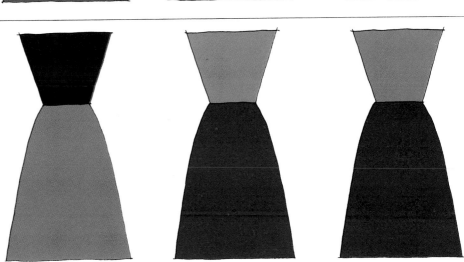

1. 大人ぽい色あいでメルヘンチックなハーモニー。

2. 甘くやさしい配色に、背のびをした可愛らしさがある。

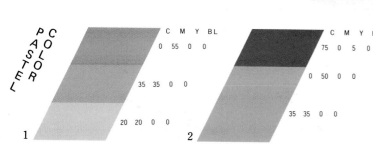

		C	M	Y	BL				C	M	Y	BL
		0	55	0	0				75	0	5	0
		35	35	0	0				0	50	0	0
		20	20	0	0				35	35	0	0

1
Romantic harmony with adult tones.

2
In the sweet delicate color scheme there looks a dream of charming girl who longs for being a lady.

P A S T E L
C O L O R

1.甘い3色配色。夢と楽しさがあるメリー
　ゴーランド。

2.野原の若草のいぶきを感じる配色。

3.活発な動きを感じる、春のいぶきの色あい。

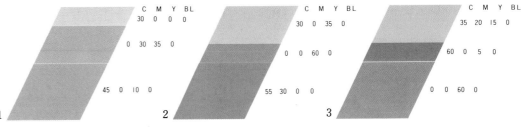

	C	M	Y	BL
	30	0	0	0
	0	30	35	0
	45	0	10	0

1

	C	M	Y	BL
	30	0	35	0
	0	0	60	0
	55	30	0	0

2

	C	M	Y	BL
	35	20	15	0
	60	0	5	0
	0	0	60	0

3

Charming 3-color scheme. A dream-like and fun folicking merry-go-round.

A color scheme with the breath of young wild flowers in the field.

Tones with the breath of spring giving the feeling of brisk movement.

	C	M	Y	BL
	0	40	5	0
	25	45	0	0
	25	45	0	0
	0	40	5	0

1

	C	M	Y	BL
	0	0	35	0
	70	0	40	0
	50	0	50	0

2

	C	M	Y	BL
	40	0	0	0
	0	0	50	0
	40	40	0	0

3

A color scheme bringing sweetness & delicacy to the hilt. The light violet gives a little touch of a young miss.

Combination of light colors. Gives the impression of the young buds in spring.

Naïve neutral color scheme.

1.あくまでも甘く優しい配色。薄紫がちょっぴりヤングミセス感覚。
2.ライトカラーの組み合わせ。春の芽ばえを感じさせる。
3.ナイーヴで中性的配色。

1.ドラマが生まれそうな優雅な色の組み合わせ。

2.ソフトな色あいが優雅でモダン。

	C	M	Y	BL			C	M	Y	BL
	35	30	0	0			0	0	35	0
	0	0	35	0			25	20	35	0
1	50	35	20	0		**2**	50	45	60	0

Exquisite and dramatic color combination.　　*Soft color tones graceful as well as modern.*

	C M Y BL
	70 0 95 0
	0 100 15 0

1

	C M Y BL
	0 100 55 0
	0 0 85 0
	100 50 0 0

2

	C M Y BL
	95 45 0 0
	0 65 90 0
	80 55 0 0

3

1. 鮮やかな色の組み合わせ。軽快で爽やかな
   ヤングカラー。
2. 原色を大胆に使った、パンチのある配色。
   ヤングカラー。
3. 静かな色あいに、からし色がきき色。セパ
   レーション効果。

Brilliant color combination. Fresh and light colors.

A color scheme with punch boldly using primary colors. Young colors.

In serene tones the mustard color is the strongest. Separation effect.

1. スポーティブエレガンス。
2. 大人のドラマチックな気分がある。おしゃれカラー。
3. 人工的な鮮やかな配色。思いきり大胆に。

	C	M	Y	BL
	5	100	0	0
	70	45	35	0
	90	0	30	0

1 *Sporty elegance.*

	C	M	Y	BL
	25	15	10	0
	65	25	25	0
	0	10	100	0

2 *A feeling of adult dramatics. Dressy color.*

	C	M	Y	BL
	5	100	0	0
	60	40	25	0
	100	65	0	0

3 *Artificially brilliant color scheme. Daringly bold.*

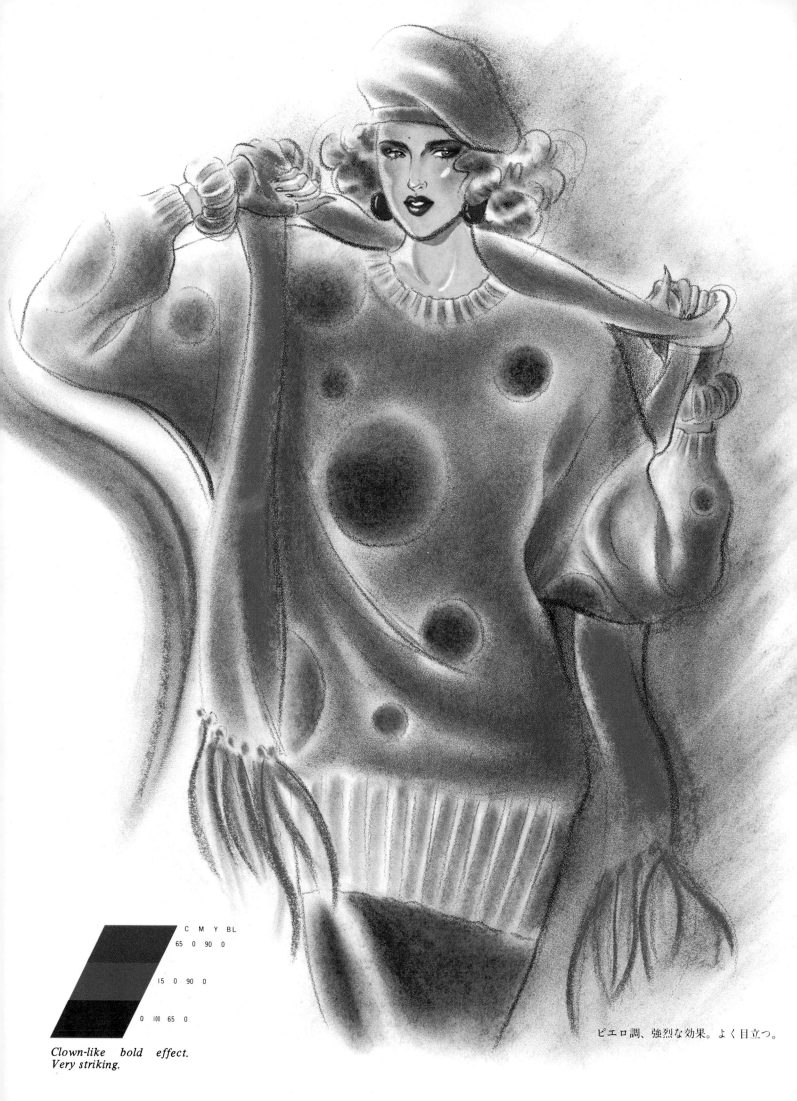

ピエロ調、強烈な効果。よく目立つ。

C	M	Y	BL
65	0	90	0
15	0	90	0
0	100	65	0

Clown-like bold effect.
Very striking.

1.ナチュラルな色味に、草色を配してアクセント。

2.類似配色が軽快で爽やかなヤングカラー。

	C	M	Y	BL
	95	5	40	0
	70	5	85	0
	75	70	0	0

	C	M	Y	BL
	0	90	0	0
	0	90	90	0
	30	15	95	0

Accent with distribution of verdure over natural colors.

Affinitive colors are light while fresh, casual colors.

GRAY-SH

	C M Y BL
	20 30 55 0
	35 70 85 15
	40 35 55 45

1

	C M Y BL
	40 60 25 0
	45 55 75 40

2

	C M Y BL
	30 25 35 10
	70 75 40 0
	85 50 20 10

3

Formal type. Serene where age doesnot matter. The brown is a quiet elegance.

Classic color. Light violet is impressive garnishing with a sweet gentleness.

British tone. Widely used from formal to casual.

1.フォーマルタイプ。落ち着きがあり年令を問わない。茶色が閑静なおしゃれを。

2.クラシックカラー。薄紫色が甘い優しさをそえ印象的。

3.英国調子。フォーマルからカジュアルまで、広範囲に使われる。

1. 渋味のあるなじみよい配色。アダルト感覚。
   イタリアンカラー。

2. 色をおさえた自由配色。自然で穏やかなカ
   ントリー調。

3. 上品な甘さと渋さがあり安定感。アダルト
   なエレガントカラー。

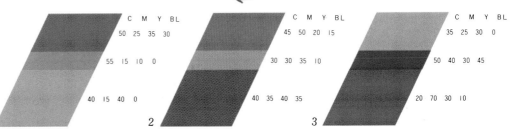

	C	M	Y	BL
	50	25	35	30
	55	15	10	0
	40	15	40	0

1

	C	M	Y	BL
	45	50	20	15
	30	30	35	10
	40	35	40	35

2

	C	M	Y	BL
	35	25	30	0
	50	40	30	45
	20	70	30	10

3

Well-adapted color scheme with a violet flavor. Adult feeling. Italian color.

Free color scheme subduing the colors. Natural and serene country feeling.

A stable feeling with refined charm and soberness. Elegant color for adults.

	C	M	Y	BL
	35	55	30	0
	35	35	40	0
	50	30	0	0

	C	M	Y	BL
	20	55	20	0
	40	35	30	0

1

Pale sober colors. Refined Japanese image.

2

Serene Japanese mood. Pink is the strongest color and together it has adult tones.

1. 淡く渋い色。上品な和風イメージ。
2. 落ち着きのある和風ムード。ピンクがきき色で、一味大人ぽい。

1. 調子のやわらかい類似色。ベルトのグレー
　がきかせ色。
2. メンズカジュアル風。落ち着いた甘さ。

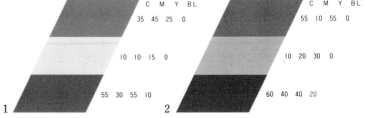

	C	M	Y	BL
	35	45	25	0
	10	10	15	0
	55	30	55	10

	C	M	Y	BL
	55	10	55	0
	10	20	30	0
	60	40	40	20

1 *Mood of soft affinitive colors. The gray of the belt is an effective color.*

2 *Men's casual. Serene charm.*

C	M	Y	BL
45	100	5	0
65	50	35	55
35	35	40	35

	C	M		BL
	40	90	20	50
	25	20	40	10
	95	80	25	30

1.落ち着いたピンクが、シックなモダンさを
　出している。個性的。
2.英国調で粋な組み合わせ。ライラック色が
　個性的。

1
*The placid pink produces a
chic modern look.*

2
*British tone—stylish com-
bination. Lilac color produces individual look.*

1. どこか古典的。ユニフォームタイプ。渋味
   の中に躍動感覚。

2. 深味とコクが強調され、エレガントな秋を
   感じさせる。

3. 反対色を渋く使っているので、縞が効果的。
   ヤングアダルト。

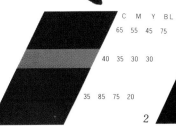

	C	M	Y	BL
	65	55	45	75
	40	35	30	30
	35	85	75	20

1

	C	M	Y	BL
	90	45	25	35
	0	0	0	100
	45	70	60	70

2

	C	M	Y	BL
	100	50	80	60
	50	40	35	50

3

In some respects classical. Uniform type. While sober it produces vibrant sensations.

Deepness and richness are emphasized. Gives an elegant autumn feeling.

As contrast colors are soberly used, the stripes are effective. Young adult.

	C	M	Y	BL
	60	100	30	45
	40	45	45	50
	55	50	45	60

	C	M	Y	BL
	50	50	60	55
	35	85	30	50
	90	70	30	25

1

Elegant autumn color. Produces a classical roman effect.

2

Chic and wooly feeling. Refined and intellectual.

1.秋のエレガントカラー。古典的ロマンを感
　じる。

2.シックでウールの感覚。上品で理知的。

1.同系色はナチュラルでまとめやすい。大人の感じ。

2.モダンでクラシックな色づかいは、どこか甘さが感じられる。

	C	M	Y	BL
	40	35	40	35
	55	40	55	15
	55	35	45	45

	C	M	Y	BL
	45	40	50	55
	25	65	20	15
	90	30	25	40

1
Juxtaposed colors are natural and easy to combine. Adult feeling.

2
The modern while young color combination produces somehow a charming aspect.

MONOTONE

	C	M	Y	BL
	40	35	30	10
	100	0	60	0
	60	50	40	80

1

Classic serene adult image.

	C	M	Y	BL
	60	50	40	80
	5	95	75	0
	35	30	30	35

2

Vivid colors used against dark colors is a point to bring out individualism.

	C	M	Y	BL
	35	35	40	35
	25	0	15	0
	20	95	75	5
	60	50	40	80

3

Orthodox dark color scheme. The red tie and pink chest gives a classy individualistic look.

1. クラシックで落ち着いた大人のイメージ。
2. ダークカラーにビビッドな色をポイントに個性的。
3. オーソドックスなダークカラーの配色。赤のタイと胸のピンクが個性的なおしゃれ感覚。

無彩色の組み合わせが、落ち着いた中にも華やかさがある。

	C	M	Y	BL
	60	50	45	80
	50	35	30	40

Noncolor combinations are serene as well as gorgeous.

繊細で柔らかい調子、全体に暗く沈んだシックなモノトーン。

*Delicate and soft. Overall
a chic monotone.*

1.ドラマチックな美しさがある。
2.ゴージャスな雰囲気が感じられる粋な色の
　組み合わせ。

	C	M	Y	BL
1	0	100	0	10
	60	50	40	80

	C	M	Y	BL
2	90	5	45	0
	60	50	40	80

There is a dramatic beauty.

A stylish color combination producing a gorgeous mood.

カラーチャート

カラー印刷する時に、赤、青、黄の３原色にスミを加え、この４色で殆どの印刷が出来ます。この４色のパーセントによって色が異なります。印刷をする時にこのカラーチャートを参考にして下さい。

※印刷インキのメーカーによって多少色が違います。

C＋M

C(0→100%)　　M(0→100%)　　Y(0%)　　BL(0%)

	100	80	60	40	30	20	10
	100 — — —	80 — — —	60 — — —	40 — — —	30 — — —	20 — — —	10 — — —
10	100 10 — —	80 10 — —	60 10 — —	40 10 — —	30 10 — —	20 10 — —	10 10 — —
20	100 20 — —	80 20 — —	60 20 — —	40 20 — —	30 20 — —	20 20 — —	10 20 — — 20
30	100 30 — —	80 30 — —	60 30 — —	40 30 — —	30 30 — —	20 30 — —	10 30 — 30
40	100 40 — —	80 40 — —	60 40 — —	40 40 — —	30 40 — —	20 40 — —	10 40 — 40
60	100 60 — —	80 60 — —	60 60 — —	40 60 — —	30 60 — —	20 60 — —	10 60 — 60
80	100 80 — —	80 80 — —	60 80 — —	40 80 — —	30 80 — —	20 80 — —	10 80 — 80
100	100 100 — —	80 100 — —	60 100 — —	40 100 — —	30 100 — —	20 100 — —	10 100 — — 100 —

C＋M＋Y

C(0→100%)　　M(0→100%)　　Y(100%)　　BL(0%)

	100	80	60	40	30	20	10
	100 — 100 —	80 — 100 —	60 — 100 —	40 — 100 —	30 — 100 —	20 — 100 —	10 — 100 — — 100 —
10	100 10 100 —	80 10 100 —	60 10 100 —	40 10 100 —	30 10 100 —	20 10 100 —	10 10 100 — 10 100 —
20	100 20 100 —	80 20 100 —	60 20 100 —	40 20 100 —	30 20 100 —	20 20 100 —	10 20 100 — 20 100 —
30	100 30 100 —	80 30 100 —	60 30 100 —	40 30 100 —	30 30 100 —	20 30 100 —	10 30 100 — 30 100 —
40	100 40 100 —	80 40 100 —	60 40 100 —	40 40 100 —	30 40 100 —	20 40 100 —	10 40 100 — 40 100 —
60	100 60 100 —	80 60 100 —	60 60 100 —	40 60 100 —	30 60 100 —	20 60 100 —	10 60 100 — 60 100 —
80	100 80 100 —	80 80 100 —	60 80 100 —	40 80 100 —	30 80 100 —	20 80 100 —	10 80 100 — 80 100 —
100	100 100 100 —	80 100 100 —	60 100 100 —	40 100 100 —	30 100 100 —	20 100 100 —	10 100 100 — 100 100 —

COLOR CHART

When printing color, black is added to the three primary colors of magenta, cyan and yellow. Almost all printing can be carried out with these four colors. The hues vary according to the ratios of the four colors. Please refer to the color charts when printing.
Note: The colors may vary somewhat depending on the printing ink's manufacturer.

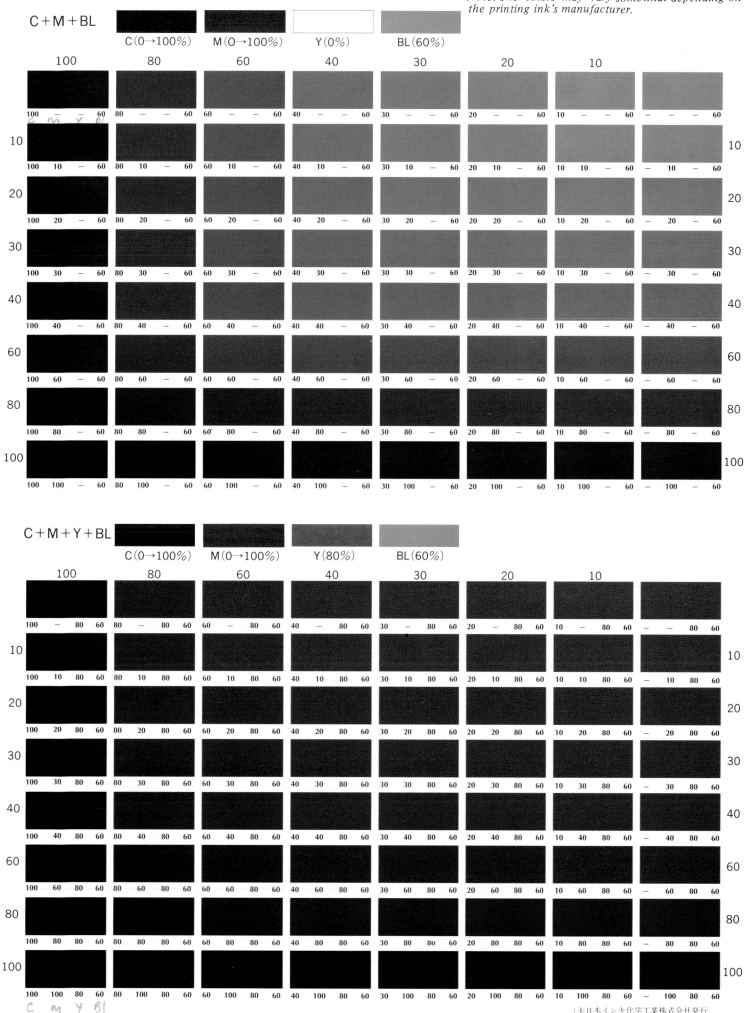

プロフィール

熊谷小次郎
ファッションイラストレーター
1941年 山形県生まれ。
22才の時に絵を描きたい一心で上京。デザイン学校でグ
ラフィックの勉強をし、グラフィックデザイナーとして
仕事についたが、自分の本当にやりたい仕事ではないと
思い、自分の求めるものを模索している時に、原雅夫ス
タイル画教室を知り、ファッションイラストレーション
を描くきっかけになり、その教室で知り合った仲間達と
SUNデザイン研究社を設立。1981年古巣のSUNデザイン
研究所を退社。独立、イラストレーション専門会社とし
て、アトリエ・フロム1を設立。

●アトリエ・フロム1 主宰
●熊谷小次郎イラスト教室 主宰
事務所　アトリエ・フロム1
　　　　〒150 東京都渋谷区代官山町20-1
　　　　コムト代官山
　　　　TEL(03)464-6048
イラスト協力　清水かおる
　　　　　　　吉田裕子

PROFILE
Kojiro Kumagai
Born in Yamagata Prefecture, 1941. Came to
Tokyo at the age of 22 to have some ambition
for art in his mind. Studied graphic design and
started as a graphic designer.　However, when
he felt something different with it and had
asked himself what he should do since then, he
happened to know Masao Hara Drawing course.
That was his turning point to fashion illustra-
tion.　After that, he established Sun Design
Laboratory with the friends of the Hara course.
Resigned there in 1981, established his own
office, "Atelier From One".
Head of Atelier From One.
Lectured in Kojiro Kumagai Illustration School.
Atelier From One: Comto Daikanyama,
20-1 Daikanyama-cho, Shibuya-ku, Tokyo 150
Tel. (03) 464-6048

Cooperate in illustrations:　Kaoru Shimizu
　　　　　　　　　　　　　Yuko Yoshida

ファッション & カラー

発　行　1985年6月25日　初版第1刷発行
著　者　熊谷小次郎（くまがいこじろう）©
発行者　久世利郎

印　刷　凸版印刷株式会社
製　本　凸版印刷株式会社
写　植　石井企画　プロスタディオ　M&M

発行所　株式会社グラフィック社
　　　　〒102 東京都千代田区九段北1-9-12
　　　　☎03(263)4318　振替・東京3-114345

定　価　2,500円

落丁・乱丁本はお取替え致します。

ISBN4-7661-0351-3 C3071 ¥2500E